Cushions
& Quilts

Front cover: (r) Eaglemoss/Lizzie Orme,
(tl) Eaglemoss/Steve Tanner, (bl) Eaglemoss/George Taylor

Page 1 Eaglemoss/Steve Tanner, page 3 Eaglemoss/Lizzie Orme,
page 4 Eaglemoss/Adrian Taylor, page 5 Eaglemoss/Adrian Taylor,
page 6 Robert Harding Syndication/IPC Magazines/James Merrell

First published in North America
in 1998 by Betterway Books
an imprint of F&W Publications Inc
1507 Dana Avenue
Cincinnati, Ohio 45207
1-800-289-0963

ISBN 1–55870–494–9

Manufactured in Singapore

10 9 8 7 6 5 4 3 2 1

Cushions
& Quilts

BETTERWAY BOOKS
Cincinnati, Ohio

Contents

1
Cushions

Add instant personality to a dull room
by stitching up a plump pile of richly
colored and textured cushions

2
Quilts

Warm up your home with cozy quilts and accessories
in a rainbow of designs – machine quilting lets you achieve
heirloom-quality results quickly and easily

Cushion ideas

*Piled in plump and welcoming softness on a sofa or favourite chair,
cushions fulfil a practical role in providing comfort and support. But
they can also play a starring part in the whole room scheme.*

Cushions, in all their different shapes, sizes and designs, are among the most versatile and useful of accessories. Make them big or small, round or square, plain or decorative. Sometimes a single big cushion is best for impact, or you may choose to pile a luscious mixture of fabrics together. Scatter huge comfy ones for lounging on the floor or stack a tasteful selection neatly on a chair. Strike an elegant formal touch with a tasselled bolster, or tailor a squab cushion to add substance to a cane chair: the type of cushion you choose can help define the style of the room and add character.

When creating your colour scheme, don't underestimate what you can do by adding a couple of cushions. To enliven a bland, uninteresting room in safe beige, a couple of cushions in a strong, rich shade – glossy indigo chenille, or a nubbly textured silk in rust – provide a vital spark of accent colour.

▲ *Rich relaxation The brilliance of a clutch of richly coloured tapestry and needlepoint cushions is shown to powerful effect against an austere pinstriped sofa. The viridian green of the wall behind enhances the contrast.*

Cushion collections

Plan your cushions carefully as an integral part of your room scheme. Decide on the number and size according to the style of your room and shape of your seating: for a casual, relaxed feel, a mixed group of different sizes arranged randomly on a sofa looks inviting. For a clearer, streamlined look, position one or two large ones rather than a group of small ones, or stack two or three neatly one behind the other in order of size. A square cushion turned diagonally on to one corner breaks up the regimented look of a row of identical ones.

To give big cushions a plump, defined depth, shake well and set in place, then make a dip in the top edge with the side of your hand.

▶ *Mixing it up A rich mixture of plains and prints, heightened with luxurious trimmings, brings together the wide variety of patterns used around the room in a concentrated burst of colour on the sofa.*

▼ *Hot shades The singing contrasts of tropical pinks, orange and yellow used in bold plain contrasts is pointed up by repeating the combination in a symmetrical row on the sofa.*

Colour coordinating

You can use cushions as a device for bringing together the various patterns and colours in the rest of the room and strengthening the effect of the scheme. Simple techniques like swapping piping fabric between cushions can be highly effective: one bright blue and one bright green cushion, piped in the opposite colours, enforce the two-tone point of a whole room.

You can also use cushions to blend a new item such as curtains into an existing scheme. Buy enough curtain fabric to re-cover a couple of cushions for the sofa, and edge them with a cord that matches the rope tiebacks.

Bring the different fabrics from around the room together for a clutch of cushions of different sizes and shapes, adding details like piping, borders and buttons in a strong plain colour to link all the elements.

Decorative details

Cushions offer the ideal opportunity to bring interest and individuality to a room. They are small enough not to be a disaster if your ideas misfire and can be changed or moved around the room to best effect. Details and decorative effects can set the style of the room: for a traditional look, choose tapestry cushions edged in fluffy ruche or gleaming cord, while bolsters trimmed with silky tassels complete a classical theme. For a

contemporary, upbeat look, try smothering a cushion in tiny buttons, or edging one in jumbo piping in a brilliant contrast colour; lace cord through eyelets round the edge, or fasten the top with huge fabric covered buttons.

For a pretty, period look, work floral prints into decorative patchwork or appliqué designs, adding feminine frills here and there. Make the most of your skills in embroidery or beading to

decorate tiny, jewel-like cushions to treasure – they look wonderful nestling among pristine lace cushions for a romantic bedroom.

For a global theme, there are lots of shops where you can find intricately detailed cushions, flashing with tiny mirrors or painstakingly patchworked and embroidered; turn old kelims into sturdy cushions with subtly faded rich colours to pile on a divan bed.

◀ *Coral and green* Carefully planned detailing gives accents to the soft and pretty colour scheme of this tasteful trio. A wavy border outlines one cushion neatly, its colour echoed on the silver-buttoned flap of a smaller one; a dainty silver shell completes the circular tailored squab.

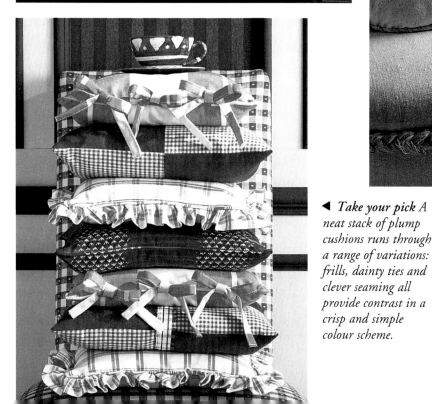

◀ *Take your pick* A neat stack of plump cushions runs through a range of variations: frills, dainty ties and clever seaming all provide contrast in a crisp and simple colour scheme.

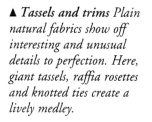

▲ *Tassels and trims* Plain natural fabrics show off interesting and unusual details to perfection. Here, giant tassels, raffia rosettes and knotted ties create a lively medley.

Shapely surprises

Unusual shapes make an interesting novelty, especially in a group. Try cutting a selection of fruity shapes – a strawberry with embroidered or beaded seeds, rosy pears and brilliant green apples, a velvety peach – to set on a plain coloured sofa. Star shapes, triangles and moons in fabrics printed with gold suns and stars would be dramatic on a dark blue sofa, and any child will love a cushion shaped and decorated like a cuddly cat or puppy.

▶ *Dream awhile The sheer indulgence of a froth of lacy pillows induces an air of romance in the most stout-hearted of souls. Snap up pieces of antique lace to concoct your own collection: vary the sizes and treatment, and add plenty of narrow ribbon and a frill or two.*

Around the home

There's no need to restrict your use of cushions to the sitting room – they can be functional and decorative accessories all around your home. Give kids' rooms a relaxing corner with a couple of huge floor cushions filled with poly beads; sculpt a layer of padding to soften wicker armchairs in the conservatory, covered in a crisp stripe. A single big cushion focuses attention on a bed – cover one in a stunning luxury fabric like a leopard print fur or rich chenille for a special touch of splendour.

Make bright and cheerful squabs for garden seats to mirror the brilliance of the flowers, for lazy days of lounging and alfresco dining. A simple bench in the hall becomes a handy telephone seat with the addition of a neat squab cushion and creates a warm, welcoming look.

◀ *Take a break Make the most of summer lounging by bringing the comfort of the sitting room out to the garden. Big cushions in bright cottons give a bench an inviting look; scatter them along a low stone wall for more informal seating.*

Bow-tie cushions

*Plump bow-tie cushions in cheerful prints or bright solids
are the perfect way to perk up a favourite chair or sofa and add a
vibrant personal touch to a whole room scheme.*

An envelope-style cover, secured with decorative ties, is one of the easiest and quickest cushion covers you can make. The cover is simply a rectangle of fabric, folded to create a pocket to hold the pad with a flap to hide it. You can make the ties in the same or a complementary fabric, or you can vary the effect by using contrasting ribbons.

A collection of easy-to-make cushion covers is a simple way of adding colour and pattern to a room. You can have fun mixing and matching plains, prints or textured fabrics to work with your existing soft furnishings. If your curtains have a rich floral print, for example, you can pick out two or three of the flower colours in plain chintz or textured cottons to emphasize the colour scheme.

▼ *Mixing and matching a variety of cover and tie fabrics in a group of cushions creates a bright contrast. Complete with jaunty bows, the ties on these cushions serve a decorative as well as useful function.*

Making a cover with ribbon ties

You can buy cushion pads in a range of standard sizes from department and home furnishing stores. To plump out the cover well, the pad needs to be 2.5-5cm (1-2in) larger than the finished cushion cover.

If you already have a cushion pad but it is a different size from the one specified here, you can still use these instructions. Just cut a rectangle of fabric the same width as your pad by twice its length plus an extra 17cm (6¾in) to allow for hems at both ends and the flap. After taking seam allowances of 1.5cm (⅝in) the cover ends up being slightly smaller than the pad.

When you are cutting out the fabric, trim away any selvedges to prevent puckering. It is also important that the corners are truly square, otherwise the cover can distort. For sewing, set your machine to a medium-length stitch.

If you want to make fabric ties to match the cover you need to buy more fabric – 75cm (30in) in total.

You will need

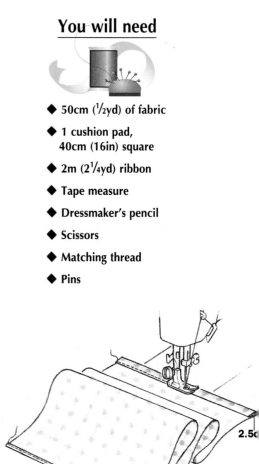

- ◆ 50cm (½yd) of fabric
- ◆ 1 cushion pad, 40cm (16in) square
- ◆ 2m (2¼yd) ribbon
- ◆ Tape measure
- ◆ Dressmaker's pencil
- ◆ Scissors
- ◆ Matching thread
- ◆ Pins

1 Preparing the fabric To straighten the cut end to 90° to the selvedges, lay the fabric on the table. Line up one selvedge with an edge of the table and check that the cut edge is straight with the adjacent side. If it isn't, hold the fabric with a book, then trim the raw edges against the table.

2 Cutting out Trim off one selvedge. Cut the fabric to a rectangle 41 x 93cm (16¼ x 36¾in) by measuring, marking and then trimming 41cm (16¼in) up from the straightened raw edge and 93cm (36¾in) from trimmed selvedge.

3 Stitching the hems On one short edge, press under 1cm (⅜in), then another 1cm (⅜in) as a double hem. On the remaining short edge, press under a 2.5cm (1in) double hem in the same way. Machine stitch along both hems, close to the inner fold.

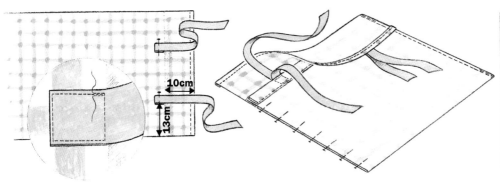

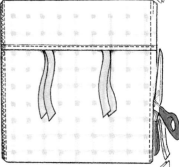

5 Stitching on the ribbons Press a crease 10cm (4in) in from the narrow hem. On the right side, pin the folded ends of the other ribbons just in from the crease, 13cm (5in) from each side, with free ends to the narrow hem. Stitch on the ribbons in a neat square round the folded ends.

6 Making the cover Right sides together, fold the cover so the wide hem lines up with the crease. Fold the remaining fabric back on top of the other layers to form the flap. Pin and stitch a 1.5cm (⅝in) seam along each side. Reverse the stitching at each end to strengthen the seam.

7 Neatening the seams Trim the seam allowances to 1cm (⅜in) and snip across the corners. Set your sewing machine to zigzag at its widest setting and medium-stitch length, and zigzag stitch along the edges of the seam allowances.

Making fabric ties

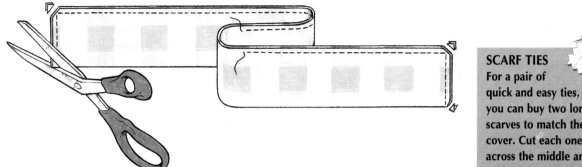

1 Stitching the ties Cut four strips of fabric 10cm (4in) wide by 44cm (17in) long. Right sides together, fold each strip in half lengthways. Taking a 1cm (⅜in) seam, stitch along all raw edges, leaving a 5cm (2in) gap in the centre of the long side for turning.

2 Neatening the strips Clip across the corners of the strip, turn to the right side through the gap and push out corners with a knitting needle. Press and slipstitch the gap closed. Stitch the fabric ties to the cover following *steps* **4** and **5** below.

SCARF TIES Tip
For a pair of quick and easy ties, you can buy two long soft scarves to match the cushion cover. Cut each one in half across the middle and neaten each cut end. Pleat up the neatened ends and attach each half scarf to the cover in the same way as the ribbons. To finish, tie off the scarves in two flouncy bows.

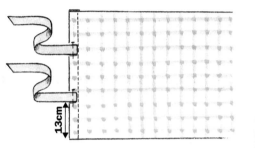

13cm

4 Positioning two ribbons Cut the ribbon into four equal pieces. Trim one end of each ribbon at an angle, then press under 2cm (¾in) at the other end. On the right side of the 2.5cm (1in) hem, measure and pin the folded end of a ribbon 13cm (5in) in from each side edge.

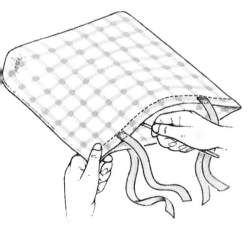

8 Turning right side out Turn the cover right side out so the flap is inside. Use a blunt tool, like a knitting needle, to push out the corners and press. To avoid straining the opening, fold the sides of the pad inwards and ease it into the corners. To finish, tie the ribbons in bows.

A toile de jouy cushion tied with filmy organdie ribbons is an elegant accessory for a handsome chair.

Making a bow-tie cover with a border

A border or flange adds a touch of elegance to a bow-tie cushion. You make up the cover in exactly the same way as the cushion on the preceding pages, cutting a larger piece of fabric. To create the border, stitch 3cm (1½in) in from the edges all round. The measurements here are for a 40cm (16in) pad.

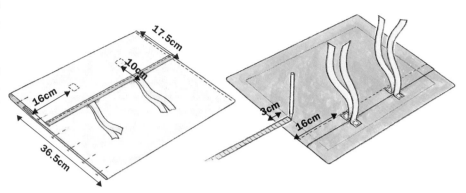

1 Cutting and hemming Cut a rectangle of fabric 47 x 105cm (18¾ x 41¼in). Hem the short ends as on page 12, step **3**.

2 Adding the ribbons Prepare and position the ribbons as in *steps* **4** and **5**, except in this case pin the ribbons 16cm (6¼in) in from each side on the 2.5cm (1in) hem. Position the other ribbons 10cm (4in) away from the 1cm (⅜in) hem, 16cm (6¼in) in from each side. Stitch all ribbons in place as before.

3 Stitching the side seams With right sides together, fold the 2.5cm (1in) hem up by 36.5cm (14¼in). Then turn the narrow hem down by 17.5cm (6¾in), aligning the 10cm (4in) crease with the wide hem. Stitch, trim and neaten the side seams as on page 13, step **8**.

4 Making the flat border Press the cushion cover well, then with a dressmaker's, pencil mark a line all round, 3cm (1¼in) in from the edge. Stitch along the line, taking care not to catch the free ribbon ends into the seam. Reverse the stitching to finish. Pad the cover as on page 13, step **8**.

For a truly luxurious effect, use moiré taffeta to make a cushion cover with a narrow border and add exotic wired ribbon bows.

Frilled cushions

*Pile on the style by adding extravagant frills to
heaps of round and square cushions for a soft, coordinating
and distinctly feminine touch.*

A bouncy halo of frilled fabric around the edge of a square or round cushion creates an instant softening effect on an otherwise plain cover. The choice of fabric, colour and width of the frill influences the overall effect of the cushion. Add a very narrow frill for a neat, modern look, or a wide, floppy frill for a more romantic effect. You can use either the same fabric as the cushion cover, or choose a complementary fabric for coordinated style.

The smartest and easiest type of frill to make is a double frill, which is a folded strip of fabric with the raw edges neatly enclosed in the cushion seam. You can add a professional touch with a row of piping between the cushion and the frill, using a matching or contrasting fabric. Alternatively, stitch a silky cord or fringe, or even a narrow lace edging, into the cushion seam as well.

For an extra frilly cushion, make two frills, one narrower than the other, and lay the narrow one on top of the wider one before gathering up. This gives you

▲ *An oversized frilly cushion adds
comfort and a light-hearted touch to a
wooden chair. By spilling over the edges
of the seat, the wide double frill acts as
both a flicked-up ruffle round the sides
and a short skirt at the front.*

the chance to use a variety of fabrics together in many different combinations.

For easy removal of the cover, insert a zip in the seam of a square cushion, where it is hidden by the frill, or across the back of a round cushion.

Making a square, frilled cushion cover

It's best to make a cushion cover slightly smaller than the pad that fills it; this way you ensure that you get a plump, well-stuffed cushion. The easiest way to do this is to cut out the cover to the same size as the pad; then, once the seam allowances have been taken up the cover will be 3cm (1¼in) smaller.

A fine row of piping defines the shape of the cushion and neatly emphasizes the softness of the frill. Use light to medium-weight fabrics if you are adding piping, as the seams can become rather bulky.

The instructions given here are for a cushion with an 8.5cm (3⅜in) wide frill and optional piping. If you want a wider or narrower frill than this, add a seam allowance to the finished frill width you want, double it and then cut strips to this measurement.

You will need

- ◆ **Furnishing fabric**
- ◆ **Square cushion pad**
- ◆ **Fabric for piping (optional)**
- ◆ **Piping cord (optional)**
- ◆ **Matching thread**
- ◆ **Zip – 10cm (4in) shorter than cushion width**
- ◆ **Tape measure**
- ◆ **Pins**
- ◆ **Scissors**
- ◆ **Dressmaker's pencil**

1 Measuring and cutting out *For the cover pieces:* measure the pad and cut out two pieces of fabric to this size. *For the frill:* measure all round the edge of the cushion and double this measurement. Cut enough strips across the width of the fabric to make up this length, when joined, by 20cm (8in) wide.

2 Attaching the piping (optional) Make enough piping to go round the edge of the cushion, plus 10cm (4in) for joining. Beginning in the middle of one side and matching raw edges, pin and tack the piping round the right side of the cushion front, clipping into the seam allowances of the piping at the corners.

◀ *Frilled cushions make an attractive and versatile addition to your cushion collection. For instructions on making tie cushions, see pages 11-14.*

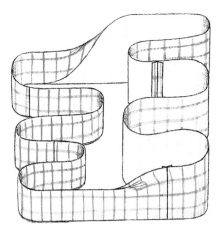

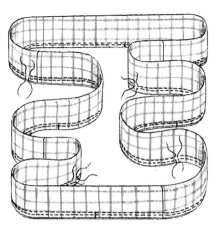

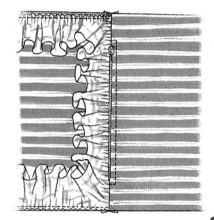

3 **Making the frill** With right sides together, join the ends of the frill strips to make a loop. Press the seams open, then fold in half with wrong sides and raw edges together and press. Divide the frill into four equal sections and mark these points on the seam allowance with a dressmaker's pencil, positioning the marks away from the joining seams.

4 **Gathering the frill** Run a gathering thread 1.2cm (½in) in from the raw edges of the loop all round, stopping and starting the stitching halfway between the four marked points. Then run a second row of gathering thread, 6mm (¼in) in from the raw edges, stopping and starting in the same places as the first row.

5 **Attaching the frill** Pin and tack the frill round the right side of the front cover piece, matching raw edges and with the marks at the corners. Pull up the gathering threads to fit and adjust the gathers evenly, allowing extra fullness at the corners. Stitch through all layers 1.5cm (⅝in) from the raw edges, pivoting around the needle at the corners. Remove the tacking.

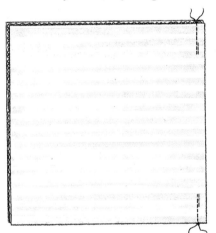

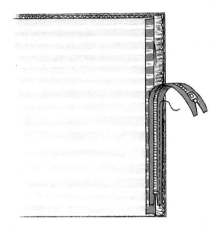

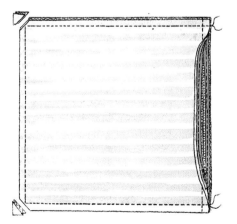

6 **Making the zip opening** Matching raw edges, lay the front and back pieces of the cushion right sides together. On one edge only, pin and stitch 5cm (2in) of the seam from each corner, backstitching at the inner ends to strengthen. Press the seam allowances open and lay the two pieces right sides together again, with the back piece on top.

7 **Stitching one side of the zip** Centre the closed zip, wrong side up over the seam allowances, with the teeth along the seamline. Pin along the right-hand tape of the zip through the seam allowances of the frill and front cover piece. Using a zip foot, stitch through all layers close to the teeth, stitching from and to the ends of the tape.

8 **Finishing the zip** Open the pieces out again, right sides up, and pin the other side of the zip tape in place under the folded seam allowance. Topstitch along the tape, 6mm (¼in) from the fold.

9 **Completing the cushion** Unfasten the zip, lay the front and back pieces right sides together again, and pin the remaining three sides. Stitch, then trim the seam allowances, clipping across the corners to reduce bulk, and neaten with zigzag stitch. Turn to the right side through the zip opening and insert the pad.

Making a round, frilled cushion cover

A round, frilled cushion cover is made up in much the same way as a square one. You can put a zip in the seam, as described on the previous page, but you may find it easier to insert the zip across the back of the cushion. The following instructions show how to do this on a round cushion with an 8.5cm (3⅜in) wide frill and optional piping.

You will need

- ◆ Furnishing fabric
- ◆ Round cushion pad
- ◆ Paper for template
- ◆ Ruler and pencil
- ◆ Fabric for piping (optional)
- ◆ Piping cord (optional)
- ◆ Matching thread
- ◆ Zip – 5cm (2in) shorter than cushion diameter
- ◆ Tape measure
- ◆ Pins
- ◆ Scissors
- ◆ Dressmaker's pencil

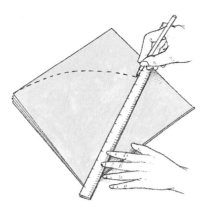

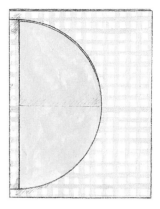

1 Making a circular template Measure the diameter of the cushion and halve it to find the radius. Fold a large piece of paper in half, then half again. From the folded point, use a ruler to measure the radius along one fold and mark. Pivoting the ruler on the point, mark off the same length all round a quarter circle at regular intervals. Join the marks in a smooth curve. Cut along the line and open out the template.

3 Attaching the piping (optional) Make piping and tack round the right side of the cushion front, matching raw edges and clipping into the seam allowances of the piping at regular intervals, as described in *Making a square, frilled cushion*, step **2** on page 16.

5 Attaching the frill Fold the cushion front in half and then in half again and mark the edges of the folds for positioning guides. Match the marks on the frill to the marks on the cushion front. Gather up the frill, adjusting the gathers evenly, and stitch around the edge of the cushion front, as described in step **5** on the previous page.

6 Inserting a zip Place the two back cushion pieces right sides together and tack 1.5cm (⅝in) in from the straight edges. Stitch 2.5cm (1in) in from each curved edge along tacked line. Open fabric out, wrong side up, and press seam allowances open. Centre zip right side down over seam and stitch along both tapes through all thicknesses. Remove tacking.

◀ *The easiest option is to make a double frill in the same fabric as the cushion cover.*

2 Cutting out Use the template to cut out a circle of fabric for the cushion front. Fold the template in half and fold the fabric for cushion back in half. Lay the template on top of the fabric, positioning the folded edge of the template 1.5cm (⅝in) away from the fabric fold, and pin. Use a dressmaker's pencil to extend the line of the template to the fold. Cut around the template, remove the pins, then cut along the fabric fold.

4 Making the frill Measure cushion's circumference; cut strips of fabric and make a frill twice this length, following steps **1**, **3** and **4** on the previous pages.

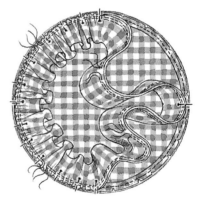

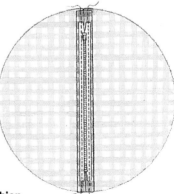

7 Completing the cushion Undo the zip, lay front and back pieces right sides together and pin round the edges. Stitch, then trim the seam allowances and neaten with zigzag stitch. Turn to the right side through the zip opening and insert pad.

Cushions with applied frills

An applied frill gives a cushion a flourish of luxury. It softens the outline and adds rich detail with intricate ruching at the inner edge.

Frilled cushions have a wonderfully frivolous, feminine look, and the ones with applied frills are the prettiest of all. Rather than being caught in the seam like a set-in frill, an applied frill is sewn directly to the right side of the fabric on the cushion front, a little way in from the outer edge.

You can make the frill as a single layer, with tiny hems on each edge; you'll find step-by-step instructions for this version over the page. Alternatively, for a smarter, more tailored finish, make a doubled frill from a strip of folded fabric, and bind the raw inner edges in a contrast or toning fabric.

▲ *Go for the gold by trimming a round cushion with an applied frill. The look is rich and luxurious, and makes a change from the usual set-in frill. The applied frill shown here is made as a single layer.*

Making a cushion with an applied frill

The applied frill on this cushion is made from a strip of fabric hemmed on both edges. For a professional finish, keep the hems as small and neat as possible. To make it easy to remove the cushion pad, a zip is sewn into the back of the cover. The instructions here are for a round cover with a 7cm (2¼in) deep frill.

You will need

- ◆ **Furnishing fabric**
- ◆ **Fabric for frill**
- ◆ **Round cushion pad**
- ◆ **Paper for template**
- ◆ **Ruler and pencil**
- ◆ **Matching thread**
- ◆ **Zip – 5cm (2in) shorter than cushion diameter**
- ◆ **Tape measure**
- ◆ **Scissors**
- ◆ **Pins**
- ◆ **Dressmaker's pencil**

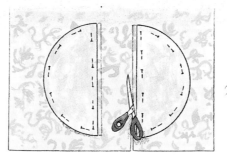

1 Cutting the back and front Make a template for the cushion as on page 18, step **1**. Cut the cushion front from this. Then cut the template in half and use the two pieces to cut the back, adding 1.5cm (⅝in) to each straight edge and matching the pattern if necessary.

2 Cutting the frill Measure round the circumference of the cushion and multiply by two for the total frill length. Cut enough 9.5cm (3¾in) wide strips of frill fabric to make up the total length required.

▼ *For a more tailored look on a square cushion, fold the frill strip double and enclose the raw edges in a narrow contrast binding before gathering up the frill – this technique gives smart emphasis to the inner ruched edge.*

3 Making the frill Use flat-fell seams to join the strips to make a loop. On each raw edge, stitch a double 6mm (¼in) hem. Fold the frill into quarters and mark with pins along one edge. Mark a line 2cm (¾in) in from this edge. Work two rows of gathering threads all round, one on each side of the marked line, breaking at the pins.

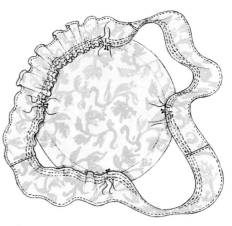

4 Applying the frill Mark a line on right side of cushion front, 4cm (1½in) in from the edge; divide it into quarters and mark with pins. Pin wrong side of frill to right side of cushion front, matching pins and marked lines and pulling up the gathers to fit. Stitch together along marked line.

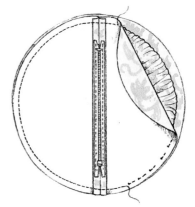

5 Completing the cushion Join the two halves of the back and insert the zip as on page 18, step **6**. Pin outer edge of frill to the centre of the cushion front to avoid catching it in the seam. Complete the cushion as in step **7**.

Basic piped cushion

*For a smart, neat accessory to complement
any room scheme and add a touch of comfort,
a piped cushion is perfect every time.*

A well-made piped cushion is one of the classics of soft furnishings. It can fit into any room design, whether modern or traditional, simple or decorative, and always adds a sense of welcoming comfort. Its versatility is great fun – you can play at colour mixing-and-matching with a clutch of different colours and patterns, switching them between the fabric and piping to create a really interesting look.

Inserting the zip in the side seam means that the cushion is presentable from both sides – you could use different fabrics for each side if you wish, and alternate to suit your mood.

Suitable fabrics

Any mediumweight, woven fabric is suitable for turning into a piped cushion. Very fine or soft fabrics may show the texture of the piping cord; you can avoid this by using a double layer of fabric or a lining underneath when making the piping. Pile fabrics like velvet work well; if you want to use a heavier fabric – perhaps to make up a piece of tapestry into a cushion – choose a more flexible fabric for the piping in a toning colour.

A single 36cm (14in) square or round cushion cover can be made from 50cm (½yd) of fabric, so save any scraps of a suitable size you have left over from other projects, and browse through the remnant tables in the shops.

Buying piping cord

Match your piping cord carefully to the style and fabric of the cushion. For a neatly tailored, subtle finish to the cushion, choose a narrow cord and cover it in the same fabric as the cushion. If you want to make a bolder statement, choose a thicker cord to emphasize the contrasting fabrics. You can buy jumbo piping cord in some shops – this is a little more difficult to work with, but it adds strong character detail to a cushion.

Buy enough piping cord to go all round the sides of the cushion plus 10cm (4in) for joins. If you are going to wash the cover, make sure you buy pre-shrunk piping cord.

Buying a zip

The zip should be about 7.5cm (3in) shorter than the cushion width. Choose a mediumweight zip in a colour that matches the main fabric.

▶ *A simple, neatly piped edge gives a crisp finish to a stack of cushions in subtly mixed textures and plains. Self-piping is the perfect understated finish for a cover.*

Piping a cushion cover

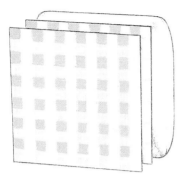

1 Cutting out For the front and back, cut two pieces of fabric exactly the same size as the cushion pad, without any extra for seams (this ensures that the final cushion is plumply stuffed).

2 Preparing the piping To decide on width of bias strips, wrap the fabric round the piping cord and add 4-4.5cm (1½–1¾in). Cut out bias strips to this width and long enough to go all round cushion plus 10cm (4in).

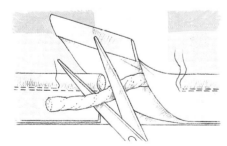

3 Adding the piping Right sides and raw edges together and starting in the middle of one edge, pin piping to front piece. Clip piping seam allowance at corners so that it lies flat. Stitch, leaving 5cm (2in) loose at each end.

4 Joining piping Unpick stitching on first end of piping; trim back cord so it butts up against the other end when laid flat. Trim fabric at an angle to stagger the thicknesses, and fold under 1cm (⅜in). Lap this end of fabric round remaining end; pin and stitch.

5 Preparing the zip seam Right sides together, pin equal amounts of the seam at top and bottom edges on one side of the cushion, leaving a centred space exactly the length of the teeth of the zip. Stitch the seam, reversing at ends to strengthen. Press the piping seam allowances towards the back piece, and lay the pieces right sides together again.

6 Adding zip Centre the zip, wrong side up, on the opened seam allowances, with the teeth along the seamline. Pin along the right hand side of the tape, close to the teeth. With a zip foot attached, stitch from one end of the tape to the other.

7 Completing the zip Open the pieces out again, right sides up, and pin the other side of the tape in place under the folded seam allowance. Topstitch from one end of the tape to the other, 6cm (¼in) from the folded edge.

▶ *For instant impact on a pair of contrasting cushions, switch the colours of the piping and a large central button to draw a vibrant link between the two.*

You will need

- ◆ Main fabric
- ◆ Piping fabric
- ◆ Cushion pad
- ◆ Piping cord
- ◆ Zip
- ◆ Matching thread
- ◆ Tape measure, pins

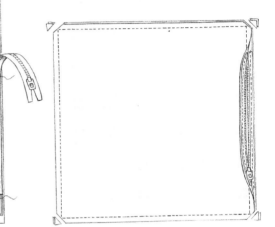

8 Finishing off Unfasten the zip. With right sides together and raw edges matching, stitch round the three remaining sides. Trim the seam allowances and clip the corners. Zigzag or oversew edges to neaten. Turn to right side; insert pad.

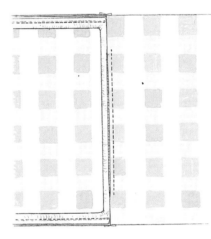

Easy bolster cushion

Bolsters have a wonderfully smart, tailored look, and add a style all their own — and they are surprisingly easy to make.

The distinctive rolypoly shape of a bolster gives a formal, dressed up look to almost any setting. Make one that fits across your bed, and pile coordinating cushions in front of it for luxurious, Cleopatra-style reclining. In the living room, place a bolster at each end of a plain sofa for an air of elegance; or in a teenager's room, use bolsters to turn a plain divan bed into a stylish day bed or sitting area.

The bolster cover has a gathered end which you can finish with a button, a fabric rosette or a stunning tassel. You could use a different fabric for the end, such as a plain to highlight a stripe in the main section. The cover has a zip to make it easy to remove for washing.

▼ *This bolster is trimmed with thick cord, and sumptuous matching tassels. Use flanged cord in the same way as piping, or stitch on ordinary cord by hand after completing the cover.*

Making the bolster cover

You can buy feather or synthetic-filled bolster pads in standard sizes from department stores, or order a made-to-measure pad from a foam supplier.

You will need

- ◆ Bolster pad
- ◆ Furnishing fabric for main section and end sections
- ◆ Matching thread
- ◆ Zip – 10cm (4in) shorter than the bolster
- ◆ Two self-cover buttons
- ◆ Contrast fabric for piping
- ◆ Piping cord to go twice round the bolster plus 20cm (8in)

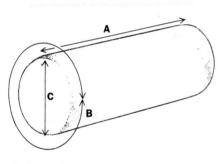

1 Measuring up and cutting out
For the main section, measure the length (**A**) and circumference (**B**). Add 3cm (1¼in) to each measurement and cut a piece of fabric to this size. *For the end sections*, measure the diameter (**C**), halve it and add 3cm (1¼in). Cut two pieces this width by **B** plus 3cm (1¼in). *For piping*, cut enough bias strips to make a length twice **B** plus 20cm (8in).

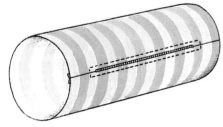

2 Inserting the zip Bring the long edges of the main piece right sides together. Pin and stitch, leaving an opening in the middle the length of the zip. Press open. Sew the zip in place.

3 Adding the piping Cover the cord with bias strips to make piping, and stitch the piping to the raw edges at each end of the main section, trimming and neatening the ends.

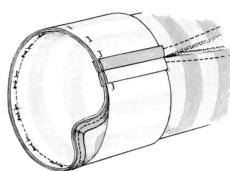

4 Adding the end sections Right sides together, pin the short edges of each end piece; stitch taking a 1.5cm (⅝in) seam. Press the seams open. With right sides together and matching seams and raw edges, pin an end section to each end of the main piece, sandwiching the piping in between. Stitch through all layers along the same stitching line.

▼ *Make a set of bolster cushions in toning fabrics, finished off with different trims. Use self-cover buttons to neaten the gathers, or buy special button-shaped trims with dangling tassels.*

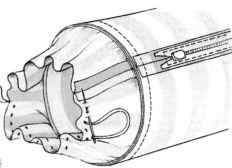

5 Gathering the ends On the wrong side of each end section, use double thread to make small running stitches 1.5cm (⅝in) in from the outer edge. Pull tightly to gather up; wind the thread twice round the bunched fabric, and fasten off.

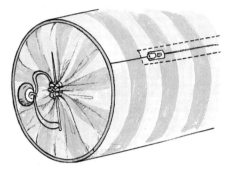

6 Finishing off Turn the cover to the right side. Cover the buttons following the instructions on the pack, and stitch a button to the centre of each gathered end.

Envelope cushions

Fastened with a single button, these cushion covers are an ingenious adaptation of a simple envelope. The designs allow you plenty of scope for creating clever effects with fabrics.

Two different ideas for envelope style cushions are given here. The first version features four triangular flaps of fabric, fastened in the centre and revealing a separate cover underneath. The second version follows the more traditional look of an envelope, with a single flap that doubles as the closure for the cushion cover.

Both styles offer you the opportunity for combining fabrics of differing colours, patterns and textures – you may even be able to use up all those offcuts and scraps you've been hoarding. Choose stripes, checks or a big swirly pattern over a plain colour, or maybe a pretty floral over a tiny sprigged cotton. Alternatively, mix and match crunchy natural fabrics in creams, beige and taupe.

The examples shown on these pages all

▲ *With an all-over fabric design such as this, you can save time by cutting the top cover out in one piece, rather than stitching on the triangular flaps separately (see the tip box on page 27).*

use buttons covered in one of the fabrics of the cover to secure the flaps. You could also use plain fabrics with one big showy button as the focal point.

Making the cover with flaps

You will need

- ◆ **Square cushion pad**
- ◆ **Fabric for overcover and undercover**
- ◆ **Lining for overcover**
- ◆ **Matching thread**
- ◆ **Self-cover button**
- ◆ **Paper, pencil and ruler to make the pattern**
- ◆ **Adhesive tape**
- ◆ **Scissors**

The instructions given here involve joining separate triangular flaps to a back section, enabling you to create interesting effects with directional fabric designs. For instance, on the cushions shown opposite, the stripes converge to meet in the centre. Alternatively, if you are using a plain fabric, or a print that does not have an obvious direction, you can follow the much quicker, shortcut method given in the tip, below right.

You are unlikely to need to remove the undercover frequently for cleaning, so it is simply slipstitched closed. For a neat finish to the outer edges, the overcover is fully lined and the four triangular flaps are fastened at the centre with a button and rouleau loop. The amount of fabric required depends on the size of the cushion pad you use.

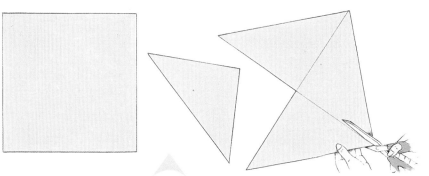

1 Making the undercover Measure the cushion pad and cut two pieces of fabric to exactly the same size. Right sides together, stitch round all four sides, taking a 1cm (³⁄₈in) seam and leaving an opening large enough to insert the pad. Insert the pad, and slipstitch the opening closed.

2 Making the overcover pattern Cut two squares of paper to exactly the same size as the pad. Use one square as back cover pattern. *For the flaps:* use a ruler and pencil to divide the remaining square into four triangles, marking diagonally from corner to corner. Cut along these lines.

3 Cutting out the overcover Lay the fabric and lining right sides together, and pin the square and triangular patterns in place. For stripes which meet in the middle, position the triangles with their long edge at right angles to the stripes. Take care to centre each point on a stripe. Cut out, adding 1.5cm (⁵⁄₈in) to the two short side edges of each triangle.

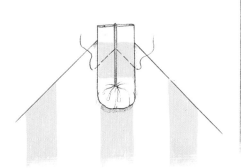

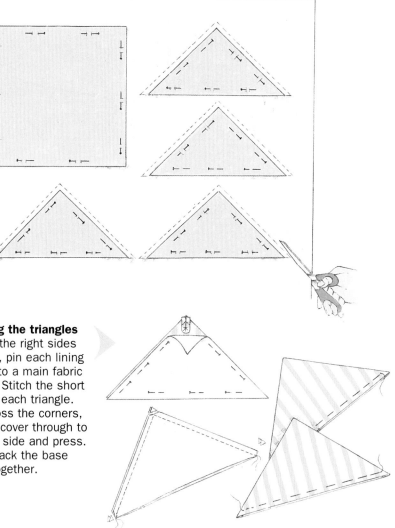

4 Attaching the rouleau loop Cut a 6 x 2cm (2³⁄₈ x ³⁄₄in) strip of main fabric on the bias. With right sides together, fold the bias strip in half lengthways and stitch the long edge, taking a 6mm (¹⁄₄in) seam allowance. Turn right side out. Then fold the rouleau loop in two and position it on the point of one of the triangles, with the raw ends towards the point.

5 Lining the triangles With the right sides together, pin each lining triangle to a main fabric triangle. Stitch the short sides of each triangle. Clip across the corners, turn the cover through to the right side and press. Finally, tack the base edges together.

▶ *Joining the triangular flaps to the cover separately ensures that the stripes have maximum design impact.*

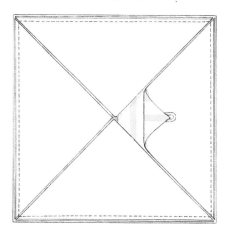

6 Joining the triangles to the back
With right sides together, lay the four triangles on top of the back cover square, so that the long raw edges of the triangles are level with the sides of the square, and the points meet in the centre. Pin and stitch all round the outer edge.

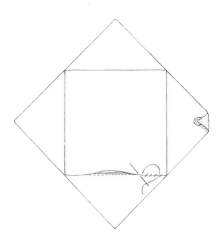

7 Adding the back lining Place the triangle section on the work surface so that the triangles are folded in and the lining side faces up. Right side down, position the back lining on top of the triangles. Pin, then stitch round outer edge taking a 1cm (⅜in) seam allowance and leaving a 10cm (4in) gap on one side. Turn to right side. Slipstitch opening closed. Press cover.

8 Completing the cushion cover
Fold in the three triangular flaps without the loop so that they meet in the centre; hand sew the points together. Cover the button following the manufacturers' instructions, and stitch it over the centre points. Insert the cushion pad and slip the loop over the button to secure remaining flap.

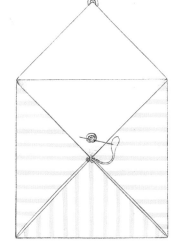

INSTANT VERSION   **Tip**
For fabrics without a directional design, you can cut the overcover in one piece. Prepare the undercover and pattern pieces following steps 1-2, then tape triangular pattern pieces to each side of square. Cut out the cover and lining each in one piece. Attach loop to one corner as shown, then simply stitch lining to main fabric around outer edges and turn through to right side.

Single flap cover

These single flapped covers are yet another clever version of the traditional envelope idea, and are quick and easy to make. While looking decorative, the flap doubles as the closure for the cover.

You will need

- ◆ **Cushion pad**
- ◆ **Fabric for cover front and back**
- ◆ **Fabric for flap and flap lining**
- ◆ **One self-cover button**
- ◆ **One press stud or Velcro spot**
- ◆ **Matching thread**
- ◆ **Paper for pattern**

1 Making a flap pattern Measure cushion pad. Cut a piece of paper to same size; then fold it in four to find the centre and mark a point about 5cm (2in) below. From top two corners, measure and mark 4cm (1½in) down the sides. From these points, draw a line down to the first mark, then cut out flap. Discard lower section.

2 Cutting the fabric *For back:* cut one piece same size as pad. *For front:* cut a piece same size as pad, plus 1.5cm (⅝in) at top edge for a hem. *For flap:* use flap pattern to cut one each from fabric and lining, adding 1.5cm (⅝in) to diagonal edges.

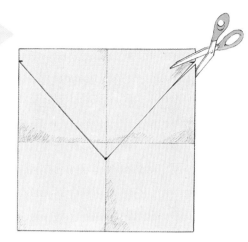

3 Making and attaching the flap With right sides of the lining and fabric together, stitch the short sides and diagonal edges. Trim the seam allowances and clip across the points; turn to the right side and press. Tack across the raw edges. Then, with right sides together, lay the flap on the back piece, with raw edges of flap level with the top edge, and leaving equal seam allowances on either side. Pin and stitch.

4 Hemming the front cover On the front cover, press under a double 1.5cm (⅝in) hem on the top edge; pin, and then stitch close to the fold.

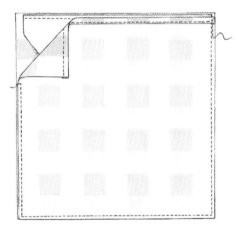

5 Assembling the cover Lay front and back pieces right sides together, sandwiching flap between. Pin sides and bottom edge together; stitch, backstitching at ends of seamline.

6 Completing cover Trim the seams and zigzag stitch all round to neaten. Turn cover right side out and press. Following manufacturer's instructions cover the button, then stitch it in place on flap. Stitch a press stud or Velcro spot underneath to fasten flap.

◀ *Have fun mixing and matching the fabrics – checks and stripes in two sizes have been used to great effect here.*

Mitred cushions

Precision cutting and careful pattern matching are the keys to making these effective cushion covers. The design is based on mitring panels of fabric together to form strong geometric designs.

A dding two or three new cushions is an easy and relatively inexpensive way to introduce a fresh look to a room – adding colour, pattern and comfort in one fell swoop. These mitred cushion covers are particularly eyecatching, and a practical way of using up fabric remnants.

A mitre is formed when two pieces of fabric are stitched together at an angle of 45°. Instructions for two types of mitred cushion are given here. The cushion shown above is made by joining four triangles of fabric across the

bias to form a square. Alternatively, you can stitch a mitred border around a square centre panel.

This device is particularly effective when using striped fabrics, fabrics with a border design, or fabrics with a strong vertical or horizontal pattern. The pattern can be matched to form a frame around the sides of the cushion, for example, or positioned to create a dramatic cross in the centre. Alternatively, you can join plain fabrics of different colours or type – such as silk and velvet – for a colour or textural contrast.

▲ *To recreate the distinctive look of this cushion cover, choose a bold, irregular stripe. The tassel, stitched to the centre of the cushion, is framed to perfection by the mitred stripes.*

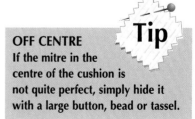

OFF CENTRE
If the mitre in the centre of the cushion is not quite perfect, simply hide it with a large button, bead or tassel.

Tip

Making a mitred cushion

Accurate cutting and sewing is vital when making a mitre, to ensure a neat finish. For a standard 40cm (16in) square cushion you need about 1m (1⅛yd) of fabric; if you want to use a particular feature of the design, such as a stripe or border pattern, you will need to allow extra fabric for positioning this.

The back of this cushion is cut as a single square of fabric. However, if you want to make the entire cushion from scraps of fabric, make the back from a second mitred panel.

▼ *Use fabric with a bold stripe to create a dramatic focal point in any room. It's essential that all the stripes match exactly to ensure neat and accurate mitres. A decorative button draws the eye to the centre of the cushion and disguises any imperfections where the four triangles meet.*

You will need

◆ Furnishing fabric

◆ Matching thread

◆ Zip, 8cm (3in) shorter than the cushion side seam

◆ Cushion pad

◆ Paper

◆ Pencil

◆ Ruler

◆ Tailor's chalk

◆ Small tassel or button for trimming finished cushion cover (optional)

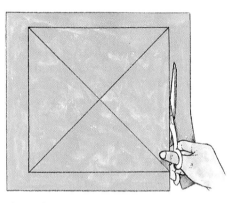

1 Making the pattern Measure cushion pad; use a ruler and set square to draw a square this size on paper. Mark two diagonal lines, from the corners, crossing in the centre. Cut out the pattern piece around square outline.

2 Cutting out back panel Pin pattern on to the fabric. Cut out one piece for back panel, adding a 1.5cm (⅝in) seam allowance all round. Then cut the paper pattern into four triangles along the marked diagonal lines.

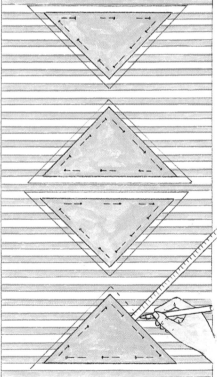

3 Cutting out the front Pin the pattern triangles on to the fabric. To match the pattern, make sure the three points of each triangle are positioned in exactly the same way on the stripes; if necessary, use a ruler to measure the distance between the stripes and the points. Use a dressmaker's pencil to mark a 1.5cm (⅝in) seam allowance round each pattern piece. Cut out each piece.

▶Mitred cushions are a good way of experimenting with different fabrics and colours. The blue and beige combination here creates a stylish, geometrical effect.

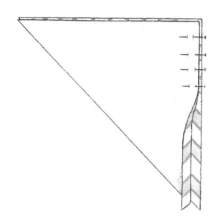

4 Matching the pattern With right sides facing and inserting the pins at right angles, pin two triangles together, taking care to match the pattern at the seams. Repeat with the other two triangles.

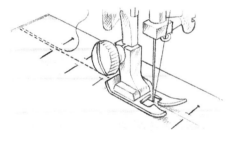

5 Stitching the seams With right sides together and backstitching at both ends, stitch each pair of triangles together, stitching over the pins. Press the seams open.

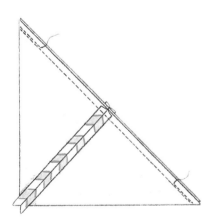

6 Completing the front Pin and stitch the pairs of triangles together, taking care to match the centre seams and pattern as before. Press the seams open.

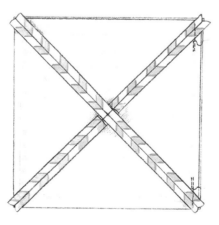

7 Inserting the zip With right sides together and matching raw edges, pin front and back together. On one edge only, stitch 4cm (1½in) of the seam from each corner, backstitching at the inner ends to strengthen. Insert the zip.

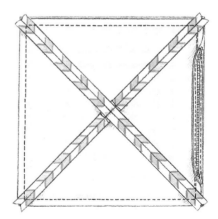

8 Finishing the cushion Unfasten zip. With front and back pieces right sides together, pin then stitch remaining three sides. Neaten seam allowances, clipping across corners. Turn to right side. If desired, use double thread to hand stitch a tassel or button to the centre of the front. Insert the pad.

Mitred border cushion

Another way of using the mitred technique is to add a wide border around a central square. Use a stripe to add a crisp edge and designer interest to a plain fabric, or frame a patterned fabric with a plain border – the choice is yours. As a guide, the border needs to be at least 5cm (2in) wide. You can increase the width to suit your fabric design and cushion size.

You will need

- ◆ Furnishing fabric
- ◆ Contrast for border
- ◆ Matching thread
- ◆ Zip, 8cm (3in) shorter than cushion side seam
- ◆ Cushion pad
- ◆ Paper, pencil and ruler
- ◆ Set square (optional)
- ◆ Dressmaker's pencil
- ◆ Pins

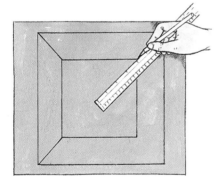

1 Making the pattern Decide on size of centre panel; use a set square, ruler and pencil to draw a square on paper to this size. From this, measure the width of the border – about 5cm (2in) – and draw a second square to this size. Mark a line from each corner of centre panel to corners of border. Cut out along outer line.

2 Cutting the pattern pieces Pin the pattern to the fabric and use a dressmaker's pencil to draw a 1.5cm (⅝in) seam allowance all round. Cut out one piece for back panel, then cut up the paper pattern to give the centre panel and four border pieces. Pin the centre panel to fabric and draw a 1.5cm (⅝in) seam allowance all round. Cut along the marked line.

3 Cutting the border fabric Pin the border pattern pieces on to the fabric, matching the design on each piece, as in step **3** on page 30. Mark a 1.5cm (⅝in) seam allowance round each pattern piece. Cut out.

4 Joining borders Place two of the border pieces right sides together, matching short and long edges; pin across one diagonal end. Taking a 1.5cm (⅝in) seam allowance and backstitching at each end, stitch from outer edge, stopping 1.5cm (⅝in) from inner edge. Press seam open. Repeat for remaining three corners of border to form a frame.

5 Adding the border With right sides together, pin the inner edge of the border to the centre panel. Stitch across each side, pivoting the fabric around the needle at each corner. Snip into seam allowances of border at each corner, just inside stitching. Neaten seams and clip corners. Open out border and press.

6 Completing the cushion Insert the zip and finish the cushion following steps **7-8**, *Making a mitred cushion*.

▲ *A mitred border is a very versatile device and can be effectively used to form a strong composition. Here, a crisp, narrow-striped border beautifully sets off a plain linen background.*

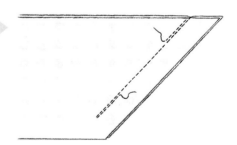

Eyelet cushions

*Add a nautical flavour to your living room
by making smart cushion covers decorated with large
metal eyelets, laced up with cord or rope.*

*Use a strong Indian
cotton or cotton canvas
for the cover. Stripes
and plains are ideal, as
the eyelet fastening is all
the decoration the cover
needs. Choose white,
blue or red for a
nautical look, or any
other colour to go with
your room scheme.*

Eyelet covers

This cushion cover has a mock laced opening. The eyelets and cord are for decoration only and the mock opening is created by folding the centre front of the cushion into a pleat. An envelope back or zip would spoil the effect, so the cover is made without an opening. When you want to launder the cover, simply unpick the side seam. It will only take a few minutes to sew it up again.

Use a plain, striped or checked fabric in firmly woven cotton, cotton drill or canvas to make the cover. You can buy eyelet kits from sewing and craft stores, mail order craft suppliers and from yachting equipment shops.

You will need

- ◆ 40cm (16in) cushion pad
- ◆ 40cm (1/2yd) of furnishing fabric
- ◆ 2.5m (2 3/4yd) of furnishing cord or rope
- ◆ 11mm (1/2in) eyelet kit with fixing tool
- ◆ Hammer
- ◆ Dressmaker's pencil
- ◆ Matching thread
- ◆ Scissors

1 Cutting out *For the cover back:* cut one 40cm (16in) square. *For the cover front:* cut one 50 x 40cm (19 3/4 x 16in) rectangle.

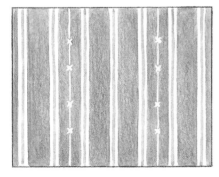

2 Marking the eyelet positions With cover front right side up, use the ruler and dressmaker's pencil to mark a line 15cm (6in) in from each short side. For the eight eyelet positions, mark 10cm (4in), then 16cm (6 1/4in) in from both long sides on both lines.

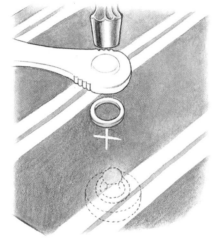

3 Fixing the eyelets Following the manufacturer's instructions, fix an eyelet at each marked position.

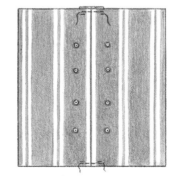

4 Making the front pleat On the cover front, measure and mark the centre of each long edge and then 5cm (2in) either side of each centre mark. To make the pleat, bring the outer marks in to meet the centre marks. Press and tack the edges.

▲ *Lace the cushion with furnishing cord; or, for authentic seaside style, use real rope bought from a yacht chandlers.*

5 Assembling the cushion cover Right sides facing, pin and tack the two cover pieces together. Taking a 1.5cm (5/8in) seam, stitch together, leaving a gap of 30cm (12in) to turn the cushion through. Turn in the seam allowances in the gap and press.

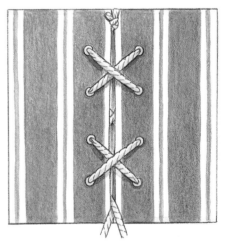

6 Finishing the cushion cover Turn the cover to the right side and insert the cushion pad. Slipstitch the opening closed. Cut the cord into two. Using the picture as a guide, lace the cord through the eyelets. Knot the ends of the cord to finish.

Cord on cushions

Furnishing cord adds a classic finishing touch to cushions. Start by making a cushion with a simple cord edging, then progress to working decorative knots and loops.

Stitching on a cord trim is a quick way of adding a finishing touch to a plain cushion. It is much easier than making up fabric covered piping from scratch and gives a bolder edging.

For design inspiration, look at the range of different cord and cord trims in the curtain trimmings department of your local department store. As well as the various trims on display, many stores offer a wide range of furnishing cord and trimmings available to order – ask to see the design books.

Many of the fabric design companies provide trimmings to match their fabrics, including cord, tassels and fringed edging. These coordinate perfectly with their fabrics and save you the time and effort spent searching in several shops for just the right shade of cord.

Traditional cords are made from silky yarns twisted into a rope. They blend

▲ *Make a cord trim more distinctive by tying a knot at each corner as you handstitch the cord in place.*

well with rich fabrics with a sheen, such as brocade, velvet and glossy chintz. Contemporary cord trims are made from smooth cotton fibres, or coarser fibres that give a textured finish. They work well teamed with textured cotton and other matt fabrics, such as slubbed linen.

Flanged cord

Flanged cords have a woven tape, called a flange. The flange is stitched into the cushion seam, in the same way as the raw edges of fabric covered piping, so very little hand stitching is needed.

The instructions given below are for making a cushion with an envelope back opening.

You will need

- ◆ **Square cushion pad**
- ◆ **Furnishing fabric**
- ◆ **Flanged cord** – measure all round the cushion pad and add 10cm (4in) to neaten the ends
- ◆ **Matching thread**
- ◆ **Tailor's chalk**
- ◆ **Ruler**

1 Cutting out the cover Measure from seam to seam across the cushion pad. *For the front of the cover:* cut one piece of fabric to these measurements. *For the back panels:* divide the width in half and add 10cm (4in). Cut two pieces of fabric to this width by the cushion length.

▼ *Why not make the cord edging a strong design feature by using a contrasting colour? These flanged cords are typical of the cords you might find in any sewing store. Choose either plain or multi-coloured cord in matt or silky textures.*

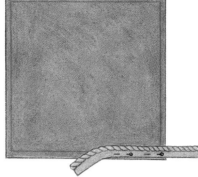

2 Pinning the cord Using the ruler and tailor's chalk, mark the stitching line 1.5cm (⅝in) in from the raw edges on the right side of the cushion front. Starting along one side, and leaving 5cm (2in) free at the end of the cord, pin the cord stitching line (where the flange and the cord meet) along the marked line.

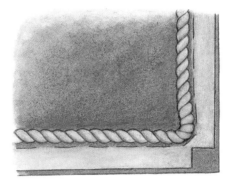

3 Dealing with corners At each corner, snip into the flange up to the cord and bend the tape around to form a right angle. Tack in place.

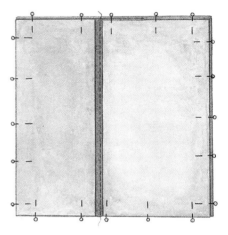

4 Joining the ends Bend the cord ends sharply down into the seam, clipping into the flange to reduce bulk, and butt them together side by side. Trim the ends to about 1.5cm (⅝in) long. Stitch together to secure.

5 Assembling the cushion On one long edge of each back panel, turn under and machine stitch a 1.5cm (⅝in) double hem. With right sides together and raw edges even, pin the two back panels to the front cover panel so that the hemmed edges overlap across the centre.

6 Stitching around the edge Pin and tack the seam, taking a 1.5cm (⅝in) seam allowance. Using a piping or zip foot, machine stitch the seam along the tacking line, as close to the cord as possible. Remove the tacking stitches and turn cover to right side.

Handstitching cord on a cushion

The instructions below are for handstitching cord around a ready-made cushion. The steps also explain how to work an optional knot or loop at each corner of the cushion. To the cord quantities given below, add about 15cm (6in) for each loop or 12cm (4¾in) for each knot.

You will need

◆ Cushion cover

◆ Furnishing cord – measure all round the cushion cover and add 10cm (4in) to neaten the ends

◆ Matching thread

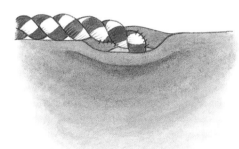

1 Starting the cord Unpick a small gap about 1.5cm (⅝in) wide in the seam of the cushion. Tuck the end of the cord inside the gap and stitch it to the seam allowance with a few neat hand stitches.

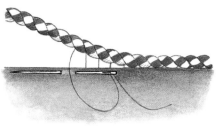

2 Handstitching the cord Stitch the cord along the seam with small, even stitches, up to the first corner. Secure the cord with a couple of extra, small stitches to hold it firmly to the corner.

3 Making a loop (optional) From the corner, measure 15cm (6in) along the cord and mark with a pin. Bend the cord into a loop so that the pin sits at the corner of the cushion and the loose end of the cord is at the front. Stitch the cord together where it overlaps with a few tiny stitches. Continue stitching the cord around the cushion, adding a loop at each corner.

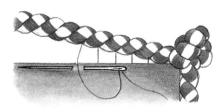

4 Making a knot (optional) As an alternative to a loop, at the first corner, tie the cord into a knot. Pull the cord so that knot lies just on the corner of the cushion, then handstitch the knot in place. Continue stitching the cord and knotting it at the corners until you get back to the start.

5 Finishing the cord Tuck the end of the cord inside the gap, crossing it over the other end slightly. Stitch it to the seam allowance and to the other cord end. Secure the gap in the cushion seam by backstitching over the stitches at either side of the gap.

▼ *The size you make the cord loop depends on your personal taste – the 15cm (6in) suggested above makes a larger loop than the ones shown here. For a loop this size, allow 12cm (4¾in) extra per loop. This cord and fabric is from a coordinating range.*

Two-tone cover trimmed with cord

This is a novel idea for a cushion cover incorporating two contrasting fabrics and a diagonal cord trim knotted at both corners. It looks great if you use a printed or patterned weave for one half and a plain for the other.

You will need

- ◆ Cushion pad
- ◆ Plain furnishing fabric
- ◆ Contrast furnishing fabric
- ◆ Furnishing cord
- ◆ Matching thread
- ◆ Ruler
- ◆ Dressmaker's pencil

▼ *Cord stitched diagonally across the front of a cushion instead of around the edge makes a striking design feature and uses much less cord. As a general guide, for a 40cm (16in) cushion pad you will need 90cm (1yd) of cord.*

1 Cutting out the front triangles Measure the length and the width of the cushion pad. *For the cushion front:* use the ruler and pencil to mark out a triangle measuring the length and width of the cushion plus 1.5cm (⅝in). Cut out. Repeat to cut triangle from contrast fabric.

2 Cutting out the back *For the back:* divide the width in half and add 10cm (4in). Cut two pieces of fabric to this width by the cushion length.

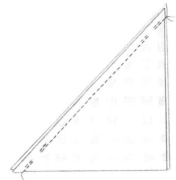

5 Adding the knotted cord Knot both ends of the length of cord, so that the cord will fit along the diagonal of the cushion with knots at each diagonal corner. Make sure you leave an end of about 5cm (2in) after the knots. Handstitch the cord to the diagonal seam, tucking and stitching the ends into the gaps in the seam.

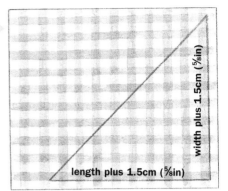

length plus 1.5cm (⅝in)

width plus 1.5cm (⅝in)

3 Stitching the front With right sides facing, pin and tack the two fabric triangles together. Stitch along the diagonal 1.5cm (⅝in) in from each end. Stitch the remainder of the seam, leaving gaps of 1cm (⅜in) either side of the initial stitching.

4 Assembling the cushion cover Assemble the cushion as for *Flanged cord cushion*, step **5**.

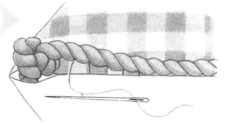

Turkish corner cushions

For a plump, sumptuous-looking cushion, try this exotic style with its softly gathered corners. Emphasize the full-bodied outline of the cushion with rich trimmings.

The deep, well-filled contours of these cushions gives them an air of luxurious Eastern romance. This effect is achieved by curving off the corners and then gathering them up, which gives them plenty of depth, rather like a squab or seat cushion.

Depending on the size you want, remember to allow for the extra depth when cutting so that you keep the breadth of the cushion in proportion to the depth. Choose a large inner pad size which will fill out the puffy shape.

There are many ways you can add interesting details to emphasize the style of the cushion. Stitch glossy cord round the seam, adding decorative loops or knots at the corners; or add contrast piping. Corner tassels, fabric puffballs or woolly pompons chosen to match your room scheme all make a perfect finish on a richly coloured cushion.

▼ *Glowing colours, damask designs and the gleam of gold accentuate the exotic, curvy lines of these cushions – choose velvets or textured silks for even more glamour.*

Making a Turkish corner cushion

These instructions are for a cushion measuring 43cm (17in) from seam to seam; when it is stuffed it will measure about 38cm (15in) across. In this version of the cushion, furnishing cord is hand-stitched along the seam and twirled into double looped knots at the corners.

The diameter of the curve used to make the pattern dictates the finished depth of the cushion. As a rough guide, allow an extra 2.5cm (1in) all round for the depth, as well as the seam allowances; buy an inner pad 2.5cm (1in) larger all round than the cut size of the cushion.

▼ *Don't waste the cord attached to the tassels – instead, stitch it round in a spiral to create a rosette for the tassel. Delicate gilt trims or tiny pompons and braid add interesting details.*

You will need

◆ **50cm (⁵⁄₈yd) of furnishing fabric**

◆ **3.5m (3⁷⁄₈yd) of furnishing cord, 1cm (³⁄₈in) diameter**

◆ **33cm (13in) zip**

◆ **Matching thread**

◆ **Inner cushion pad, 48cm (19in) square**

◆ **Seam binding**

◆ **Needle and thread**

◆ **Paper, pencil and ruler**

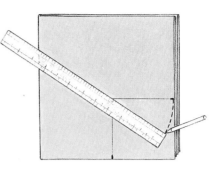

1 Making a pattern Cut a 46cm (18in) paper square and fold it in four. On the outer corner, draw a line 10cm (4in) in from each edge to form a square. Join the side marks to form a curve. Trim off surplus and open out.

2 Preparing fabric *From furnishing fabric:* use the pattern to cut two pieces. Insert the zip in one side.

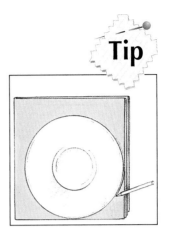

3 **Stitching the sides** Open the zip. With right sides together, pin and stitch remaining edges of the cushion, following the curves at the corners smoothly. Trim the seam allowances and zigzag stitch to neaten them.

4 **Gathering corners** Using doubled thread, run a row of gathering stitches round each corner on the stitchline, starting and finishing 2.5cm (1in) beyond end of curve. Pull up to measure 10cm (4in); secure thread.

MARKING A CURVE
Instead of plotting the curves with a ruler, find a circular object – such as a plate or saucer – 20cm (8in) in diameter, and draw round this.

5 **Securing the gathers** Cut 15cm (6in) of seam binding and centre it on one gathered corner. Pin the binding along the stitchline, adjusting the gathers; stitch the binding in place. Turn the cover to the right side and insert the pad, fluffing it out well.

6 **Tying a slip knot** Tie a single knot 28cm (11in) from one end of the cord, then push the end back through the knot to form a loop. Pull the knot tight round the loop.

7 **Forming the loops** Bring the top of the loop down to the knot to form two equal loops; secure in place with a few stitches. Trim off the cord end below the knot, and stitch through the knot with doubled thread to secure.

8 **Attaching the cord** Position knot on one corner and stitch in place. Continue stitching along seamline, making a knot at each corner. To finish, neaten cord end and secure it under first knot.

Ruched piping

Ruched piping gives the Turkish corner cushion a richly opulent look and a professional finish that's easy to achieve. The fabric strip for the piping is twice as long as the finished length required, and is cut wider than usual to allow it to ruche generously over the cord. The fullness of the gathers allows you to cut the strips on the straight of the grain.

For the cushion, you will need all the materials listed on the previous page, except the furnishing cord. For the ruched piping, you will need 2m (2¾yd) of piping cord, 20cm (¼yd) of contrasting fabric, two safety pins and a zip or piping foot for your sewing machine.

Alternatively, buy flanged cord and insert it in the same way as ordinary piping. A round puffball finished with a bead makes an interesting variation for the corners.

▶ *Give a room instant Eastern glamour with deep, puffed-up cushions trimmed in a variety of different ways. You can even change the shape of a ready made cushion with a twist of string at the corners – then add your chosen trim.*

1 Cutting out Referring to step **1** on page 40, make a paper pattern for your cushion. *From the main fabric:* use the paper pattern to cut two pieces.

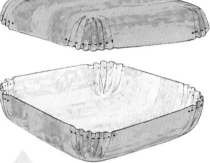

2 Gathering corners Working on front and back pieces separately, gather corners as in step **4** on previous page, ensuring fullness is equal on each corner.

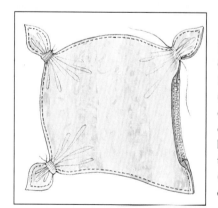

Tip

EASY CORNERS
For a quick version, use a ready-made cover. With the cover inside out, bind each corner tightly, about 2.5cm (1in) in. Then turn cover to right side.

3 Starting the ruched piping Cut enough 7cm (2¾in) wide strips of contrasting fabric to make one strip long enough to go twice round the cushion plus an extra 10cm (4in). Join the strips and press the seams open to make one complete strip to this measurement.

4 Gathering the piping Fasten a safety pin in one end of the cord. Then start making the piping in the usual way. When you have stitched about 30cm (12in), pull the free end of the cord towards you, ruching the fabric strip over it to measure about 15cm (6in). Continue in this way, repeating the process until the whole strip is stitched. Secure the free end of the cord with another safety pin. Even out the gathers, then stitch along the strip again to fix the gathers in place.

5 Finishing off Apply the piping in the usual way round the cushion front, starting in the middle of one edge and overlapping the ends to join. Then insert the zip and complete the cushion. Add coordinating corner decorations.

Shapely cushions

Give your sitting room an instant face-lift with this dazzling trio of cushions. The plump star, moon and heart shapes, outlined with crisp contrast piping, will brighten up the simplest sofa.

A batch of bright new cushions is one of the quickest and easiest ways to pep up a dull scheme or give life to a tired old sofa, and this shapely trio is no exception. With their interesting outlines – romantic heart, curvy crescent moon and eight-pointed star – they will add a distinctive touch to any room. Each one has a generous gusset to give the shape body and avoid distortion, while the piping emphasizes the sweeping lines to the full.

Make your cushions in a mixture of brilliantly coloured silks, and switch the colours round for the piping. If you prefer a more restrained look, play with an array of neutral shades, piped in jute; alternatively, try remnants of velvet or textured cottons in pastel colours.

You can have fun with trimmings; you could add a tiny pompon to each point of the star, or scatter a blue velvet moon with tiny diamonds. To play up the romance of the heart cushion, make it in shimmering red satin, trimmed with a tassel and appliquéd initials.

The cushions are designed as a team, but you could make just one or two as a gift for a friend, or create a set of plainer cushions for yourself.

▼ *A row of piping along each edge plays up the attractive shape of each cushion. Made in silk dupion, the rich contrasts of three glowing jewel colours makes the most of this stunning trio.*

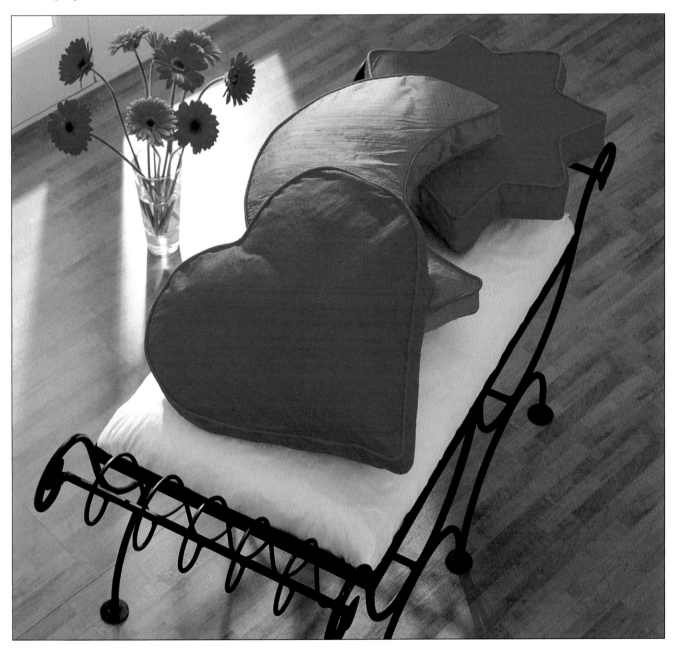

Making the cushions

Each cushion measures about 43-48cm (17-19in) across, with a 5cm (2in) deep gusset. They zip up at the back, so the back sections are cut as two separate pieces. You need 1m (1⅛yd) of fabric for each of the moon and heart shapes, and 1.10m (1¼yd) for the star.

Because of the unusual shapes of the cushions, each one needs its own inner pad to accentuate its shape. The pad is made slightly larger than the cushion cover, to ensure a plump, professional-looking fit. Make the pad from sheeting or any other finely woven cotton fabric, and use polyester or Dacron filling, from sewing and craft shops.

Take 1.5cm (⅝in) seam allowances throughout, unless otherwise stated.

heart

Traceable patterns

You will need

- ◆ **Furnishing fabric**
- ◆ **Fabric for inner pad**
- ◆ **Matching thread**
- ◆ **25cm (10in) zip**
- ◆ **2.5m (2¾yd) piping cord**
- ◆ **Polyester or Dacron filling**
- ◆ **Tracing paper**
- ◆ **Newspaper for pattern**
- ◆ **Pencil**

Preparing the patterns

1 Tracing the outlines Trace the patterns on to tracing paper, including the dotted foldlines. Mark the foldlines, then cut round.

2 Making the front patterns Cut three 50cm (20in) squares of newspaper. *For the moon and heart shapes:* fold the squares in half, and place the dashed line (marked foldline) along the fold. *For the star:* fold the square into quarters, and place each dashed line along a fold. Draw round and cut out, then unfold the patterns.

3 Making the back patterns Cut a second pattern piece for each cushion. Cut this second pattern piece in two, about 12.5-15cm (5-6in) from one edge, as shown above. These two pieces are the back patterns.

foldline

foldline

foldline

star

moon

foldline

Making the cushion cover and pad

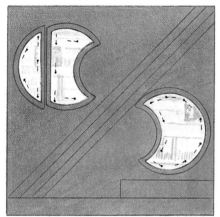

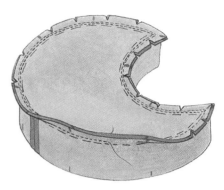

6 Inserting the zip Right sides together, stitch the straight edges of the cushion cover back pieces, leaving a gap in the middle for the zip. Press the seam open. Insert the zip.

7 Piping the edges Make up the piping. Apply round the edges of front and back, clipping seam allowances on curves and corners, and pivoting the needle at the corners as you sew.

4 Cutting the fabric *For the front and back:* pin the pattern pieces on to the fabric. Adding 1.5cm (⅝in) all round, draw round and cut out. *For the gussets:* cut enough 8cm (3¼in) wide strips to make gusset lengths as follows: star 175cm (69in); moon 153cm (60¼in); heart 141cm (55½in). *For the piping:* cut enough bias strips to make piping twice the length of the gusset.

5 Cutting the cushion pad *For the pad front and back:* using the cushion fabric front piece as your pattern, add 1.5cm (⅝in) all round and cut two pad fabric pieces. *For the pad gusset:* measure round the edge of the cushion front piece; cut enough 9cm (3½in) wide strips to go all round, allowing for joins.

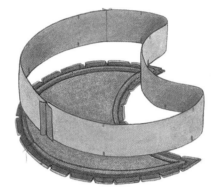

8 Preparing the gusset Join the gusset pieces to make a loop. Divide the gusset into eight to ten equal sections, marking the sections on both edges of the gusset. Measure and mark sections of equal size round the edges of the cushion front and cushion back pieces.

9 Adding the gusset Right sides together and matching the marks, pin and tack one edge of the gusset to the edge of the cushion front, sandwiching the piping; clip the seam allowances at curves and corners. Stitch, pivoting the needle at corners.

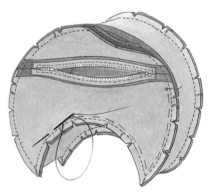

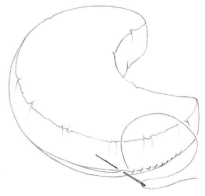

10 Completing the cover Unfasten the zip. As in step **9**, pin, tack and stitch the remaining edge of the gusset to the piped edge of the back. Trim the allowances and zigzag stitch to neaten; turn the cover to the right side through the zip opening.

11 Making the pad Pin pad gusset to the front and back sections as for the outer cover. Stitch, leaving a 10cm (4in) gap in one seam. Turn out, and stuff evenly with the filling. Slipstitch gap closed. Insert pad into outer cover.

◀ *Inserting a gusset makes all sorts of interesting shapes possible, without any danger of distortion. It's important to match the top and bottom edges carefully, for a crisp, boxy shape.*

Tucked cushions

*Give plain fabrics exciting surface
texture with simple tucking, and create three
attractive cushion covers.*

Using the tucking technique on a simple cushion breathes life into plain fabrics. It is a straightforward procedure which produces impressive results easily. Neat, straight stitching is the only skill required to produce these unusual cushion covers. They can be made from inexpensive fabrics as the tucking itself will lend an exclusive air.

Tucks can be worked in numerous ways to create exciting designs, but to start with, try the patterns created from basic parallel tucks. The texture is formed by stitching them in different directions to create intriguing effects. Mounting the cushion cover fronts on to wadding, and adding quilting on the edge of the panels, further enhances the three dimensional texture.

To create crisp tucks, choose fabrics which hold a finger-pressed crease well. Firmly woven cottons such as gaberdine or twill are ideal, while glazed cotton has a sheen, giving the finished work attractive areas of light and shade. Lightweight denim is suitable, or linen and silk which are more costly options. Avoid polyester fabric as it is springy and can be difficult to work with.

▼ *The pale, neutral colours of these tucked cushions complement the wicker furniture and allow the light and shadow effect created by the tucks to show up the three designs well.*

Making the cushion covers

The finished covers measure 38cm (15in) square. Use a sewing thread which matches the fabric, and set the sewing machine to a medium stitch length of four stitches to 1cm (⅜in). A rotary cutter and cutting mat are useful for cutting the accurate rectangles which are the starting point from which a tucked panel is created. Make sure the fabric is lying absolutely flat when marking the cutting lines and do not pull it out of shape. A set square or T-square is also useful for marking accurate corners.

You will need

For each cushion:

◆ 1m (1⅛yd) cotton gaberdine 115cm (45in) wide

◆ Matching thread

◆ 50g (2oz) polyester wadding 41cm (16in) square

◆ Dressmaker's pencil

◆ Rotary cutter, ruler and cutting mat (optional)

Making the wavy cushion cover

1 Cutting out *For the tucked panel:* cut a piece of fabric 70 x 33cm (27½ x 13in). *For the borders:* cut two strips 42 x 6.5cm (16½ x 2½in), and two strips 32 x 6.5cm (12½ x 2½in). *For the back:* cut two rectangles 40 x 28cm (15¾ x 11in).

2 Stitching the tucks Using the dressmaker's pencil, mark along both long edges of the tucked panel, at 2.5cm (1in) intervals. Finger press a fold on the first set of marks and stitch 6mm (¼in) down from the fold, using the presser foot as a guide. Continue stitching the tucks, joining the marks across the fabric and stitching in alternate directions. Press all the tucks in one direction.

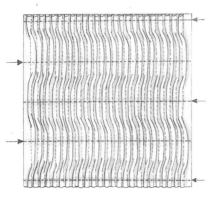

3 Forming the wavy pattern Mark 1.2cm (½in) from top and bottom edges and at 7.5cm (3in) intervals between. Stitch across the tucks on these marks, with the tucks lying in alternate directions. Make sure you hold the tucks down in front of the presser foot as you stitch so that they lie flat.

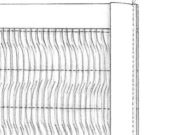

4 Stitching the borders With right sides together and matching raw edges, pin then stitch the shorter border strips to opposite edges of the tucked panel, taking 1cm (⅜in) seam allowances. Trim away any excess then press seam allowances towards the border. Repeat to add the longer border strips to the remaining edges. Trim and press again.

5 Adding the wadding Lay the cushion cover front on the wadding square and pin securely in place. Using the 'stitch-in-the-ditch' method, machine quilt round the tucked panel.

6 Stitching the back Stitch a 1cm (⅜in) double hem down one long edge of each back panel. With right sides together, pin the two back panels to the cushion cover front, matching the outer edges and overlapping the two hemmed edges. Machine stitch with 1cm (⅜in) seam allowances. Trim excess wadding, clip corners and turn right sides out. Press, then insert the cushion pad.

Making the four-patch cushion cover

This cushion cover is decorated with simple flat piping on the edge of the tucked panel. For this you will need 10cm (⅛yd) of cotton fabric in a contrasting colour.

1 **Cutting out** *For tucked squares:* cut four rectangles 33 x 16.5cm (13 x 6½in). *For borders and back:* cut as in *Making the wavy cushion cover,* step **1**. *For piping:* from contrasting fabric, cut four strips 33 x 2.5cm (13 x 1in).

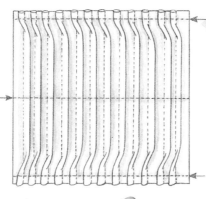

2 **Stitching the tucks** Following *Making the wavy cushion cover,* step **2**, mark the fabric and stitch the tucks on the four rectangles, then press them in one direction. Hold the tucks down with a stitched line across the centre, then twist the tucks by stitching down in the opposite direction close to the two edges.

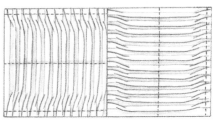

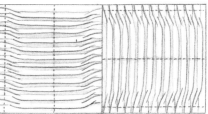

3 **Joining the tucked squares** Lay the four squares out with tucks lying in opposite directions. With right sides together and taking 1cm (⅜in) seam allowances, stitch the squares together in pairs. Then stitch the pairs together to complete the panel.

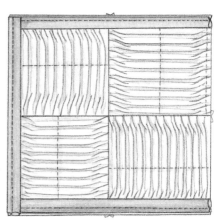

4 **Adding the flat piping** Fold contrast strips in half lengthways with wrong sides together. With right sides together and matching raw edges, pin a folded strip on opposite sides of tucked panel. Stitch in place inside the 1cm (⅜in) seam allowance. Trim away excess strip. Repeat with remaining strips on the other two edges of the panel.

5 **Finishing the cushion cover** Following *Making the wavy cushion cover,* steps **4-6**, attach the borders, add wadding, and stitch back panels.

▲ *The wavy pattern of the cushion on the left is created by stitching the tucks down in alternating directions. The central tucked panels of the four-patch cushion (above) are set off by a band of contrast piping inside the border.*

Making the honeycomb cushion cover

This is a simpler version of the wavy cushion cover, with fewer folds. It is ideal for a textured or coloured fabric, without becoming too fussy.

1 Cutting out *For tucked panel:* cut a rectangle 46 x 33cm (18 x 13in). *For borders and back:* cut as in *Making the wavy cushion cover,* step **1**.

2 Stitching the tucks Mark the long edges of the rectangle at 5cm (2in) intervals. Then stitch a 6mm (¼in) tuck at each mark across the rectangle.

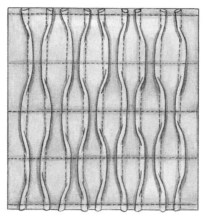

3 Forming the honeycomb pattern Mark 1.2cm (½in) from top and bottom edges then at 7.5cm (3in) intervals in between. Stitch the tucks down in pairs, alternately two facing together then two facing apart. Reverse the pattern on the next row.

4 Finishing the cushion cover Add the borders and wadding and stitch the back panels as in *Making the wavy cushion cover,* steps **4-6**.

This honeycomb pattern is a good first project if you aren't very confident about working accurate rows of parallel stitching; there are only a few tucks here, but the results are still effective.

Honeycomb smocked cushions

Smocking is a gathering and embroidery technique traditionally used for clothing, but it's just as distinctive on soft furnishings. Cushions, worked in honeycomb stitch on a check, are an ideal starter project.

S mocking is a form of decorative embroidery that dates back to the Middle Ages, when the elasticity formed by the pleats and stitches was used to add ease to work garments. The process remains an effective way of adding fullness, elasticity and decoration to clothing, in particular children's wear, and you can also apply it successfully to items of soft furnishings.

Despite the intricate-looking results, the basic steps for smocking are very straightforward. The cushions shown here are worked in honeycomb stitch – one of the simplest smocking stitches – which is pulled up to gather the fabric as it is worked. A checked fabric provides a ready-made stitching guide, so that the stitches and subsequent pleats are all evenly spaced. You can also use fabrics with other regularly-spaced patterns, such as spots or stripes.

▲ *Smocking adds a decorative touch and extra dimension to these checked cushions. You can achieve different effects by using checks of varying sizes and by the way that you position the smocking stitches on the squares.*

Materials and equipment

Suitable fabrics You can work smocking on almost any fabric, as long as it's not too stiff or slippery to handle. Evenly textured, lightweight fabrics, such as natural cotton, linen, lawn and fine wool, are the best choice. Fabrics such as gingham, or those with printed checks, stripes or polka dots are ideal, as their regular markings make it easy to achieve even gathers.

As a general guide, the smocking stitches are spaced 6-15mm (¼-⅝in) apart, so you need to choose a fabric with an appropriately sized pattern. Stitches spaced close together create small pleats, suited to fine fabrics and baby clothes, while wider spaced stitches give deeper pleats, better for heavier fabrics.

When buying the fabric, allow at least three times the width of the finished piece to allow for the gathers. Finer fabrics may require up to four times the final width.

Threads Several types of embroidery thread are suitable for working the smocking stitches, including stranded embroidery cotton, pearl cotton, coton à broder and twisted silk. Split stranded cottons into three or four strands for light or heavier weight fabrics respectively. To emphasize the smocked texture, match the thread colour to the fabric, or use a contrast colour to accentuate the stitches.

Needles Use a sharp crewel or chenille needle to work the embroidery stitches, in a size that suits the weight of the fabric and the thread.

Stitch library
Working honeycomb

You can work the honeycomb smocking by picking up the light or dark squares of the checked fabric as preferred. These instructions show the dark squares being used as a guide for the smocking.

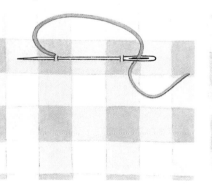

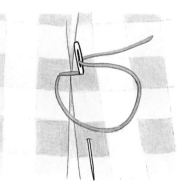

1 Stitching the top row Fasten the thread on the wrong side and bring the needle out in the centre of the first dark square. Working on the surface, on the right side of the fabric, take a backstitch into the centre of the next dark square, then take another stitch at the centre of the first stitched square.

2 Moving to the next row Pull up the thread, drawing the two dark squares together and with the light square pleated behind. Take another stitch into the centre of the second dark square and then bring the needle out in the centre of the dark square in the row directly below. Keep the thread firm but not taut.

3 Stitching the bottom row Work backstitches across two parallel dark squares in this row in the same way as before, then pull up the thread and bring the needle out in the centre of the dark square directly above.

4 Working across the width Continue along the row, repeating the smocking stitches up and down the rows across the width of the fabric. Fasten off the thread at the end of the row. Work further rows of smocking in the same way.

Smocking checked fabrics

The honeycomb technique is one of the most straightforward smocking stitches. It is worked on the right side of the fabric, from left to right. On a checked fabric it zigzags between two rows of squares. Pick up the stitches in either the light or dark squares, as desired, to produce different effects.

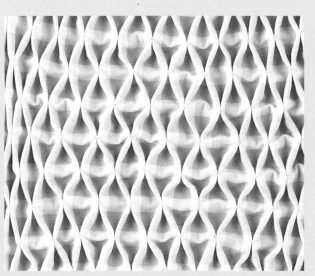

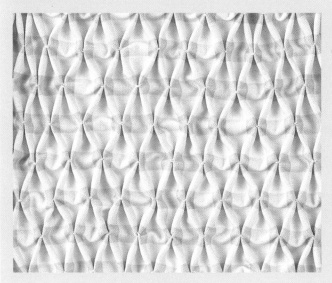

◄ *If the dark squares of a checked fabric are used as the guide for smocking, they form a distinct pattern on the surface, defined by the pale background squares.*

▲ *When the light squares of a check are used as the stitching guide, the dark squares form the background. They appear to recede, giving a lot of depth to the smocking.*

◄ *A variety of checked fabrics, in different colours and sizes, work well together to produce a highly coordinated yet relaxed look. The smocked cushion, with the smart mitred border framing the honeycomb stitching of the centre panel, adds extra textural impact to complement the room setting.*

Smocked cushion with a border

The honeycomb smocked cushions photographed on the previous pages show how you can achieve different effects by using fabric with large or small checks. The technique is the same in both cases, using a matching thread to pick up the lighter squares, but the larger check gathers up into deeper pleats. A mitred border adds a smart touch to the small checked cushion cover.

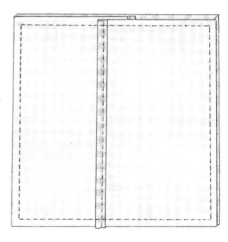

You will need

- ◆ 75cm (30in) of 115cm (45in) wide small checked fabric for mitred cushion
- ◆ 90cm (1yd) of 115cm (45in) wide large checked fabric for large checked cushion
- ◆ Stranded embroidery cottons
- ◆ Two cushion pads, 40cm (16in) square
- ◆ Matching sewing thread
- ◆ Crewel needle

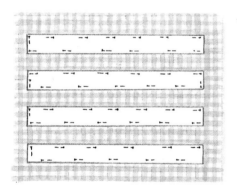

1 Cutting out the fabric Using the small checked fabric, cut out the following pieces: *For the front:* cut a rectangle measuring 70 x 50cm (27½ x 20in). *For the back:* cut two rectangles, 42 x 25.5cm (16¾ x 10in). *For the border:* cut four strips, 42 x 7cm (16¾ x 2¾in). To ensure neat, mitred corners, take care to match the checked pattern exactly on each of the border pieces.

2 Working the smocking Following *Working honeycomb,* steps **1-4**, start smocking 3cm (1¼in) in from the top left corner of the front piece. Work across the width, picking up the centres of the light squares. Continue rows of smocking down the fabric, until the smocked area measures 32cm (12½in) square.

3 Preparing the border strips Fold up one end of the first border strip diagonally and press, with raw edges matching. Unfold and cut along the crease, so the end is angled at 45°. Repeat with each end of each strip.

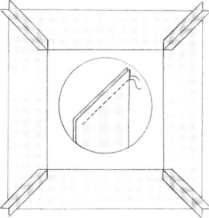

4 Joining the border strips Place two border strips, right sides together, and pin across one diagonal end. Stitch, taking a 1cm (⅜in) seam allowance and stopping 1cm (⅜in) from inner edge of border. Repeat at each end of all the strips to form a frame of fabric. Press seams open.

5 Attaching the border With right sides together, pin inner edges of border to outer edge of smocked area. Stitch together, 1cm (⅜in) from the inner edge of border. Trim the edge of the smocked panel, 1.5cm (⅝in) from the seam.

6 Completing the cushion Stitch a double 1cm (⅜in) hem on one long edge of each back piece. With right sides together and matching the raw edges, pin the back pieces to the smocked panel, overlapping the hemmed edges by 5cm (1¾in) at the centre. Stitch in place, taking a 1cm (⅜in) seam allowance. Trim the seam allowances, snipping across the corners to reduce bulkiness. Turn the cover through to the right side and press. Insert the cushion pad.

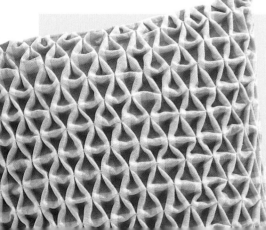

Smocked cushion without a border

From the large checked fabric, cut a rectangle 110 x 55cm (43½ x 21½in) for the front and two 42 x 25.5cm (16¾ x 10in) rectangles for the back. Work the smocked panel as before, following *Working honeycomb,* steps **1-4**, starting 4cm (1½in) in from the top left hand corner of the front piece. Continue smocking until the smocked area measures 42cm (16¾in) square. Complete the cushion cover by following *step* **6** above.

Woven ribbon cushions

Capture the opulence of luxurious ribbons by weaving them together to make colourful cushions. Add simple embroidery in bright shades to complete the eye-catching effect.

Most fabric stores are filled with a fascinating range of ribbons in a host of different colours and patterns. They come in lush velvets, luxurious silk satins, cotton, polyester and many other materials. Some have rich textures while others have wonderful patterns or colours.

Using the pictures on these pages as your inspiration, weave your favourite ribbons together to make an unusual cushion front. Some ribbons are expensive, so it is best to combine a few exotic ones with cheaper ribbons and any off-cuts that you have already.

The technique is easy. You just pin the ribbon in vertical rows to a soft board, then weave the horizontal ribbons through it. Finally, fuse the ribbon to iron-on interfacing to secure the woven pattern – it couldn't be simpler.

If you wish to create a regular pattern, like the cushion front shown above, use ribbons of equal width. However, you can achieve some exciting results using ribbons of mixed width – the pattern

▲ *This cushion front is made from woven ribbon in six coordinating colours. All the ribbons are the same type and width, creating an attractive even check.*

will look rather like tartan. Another interesting idea is to use a range of different textured ribbons. This produces a lush, exotic look, but you need to combine the ribbons carefully for it to work successfully. More ideas are shown on the following pages.

Making a woven ribbon cushion

The cushion shown on this page is 26 x 36cm (10¼ x 14¼in) and the front is made from 2.5cm (1in) wide ribbon. However, you can easily adapt the instructions to make a cushion of any size. If you wish to use ribbon of a different width, adapt your ribbon requirements accordingly – the wider the ribbon, the quicker it covers the cushion front and the less you need. You'll find it helps your calculations if you work from a rough diagram.

This cushion is embroidered with brightly coloured stars for added detail and to secure the ribbon.

You will need

- Eleven 38cm (15in) lengths of ribbon 2.5cm (1in) wide and fifteen 28cm (11in) lengths of ribbon 25mm (1in) wide in assorted colours
- 38 x 28cm (15 x 11in) rectangle of furnishing fabric for the cushion back
- 38 x 28cm (15 x 11in) square of mediumweight fusible interfacing
- Polyester stuffing or other soft filling or ready-made cushion pad
- Stranded embroidery cotton in various colours
- Crewel embroidery needle, size 7
- Safety pin
- Sewing thread in a neutral colour
- Map pins or dressmaker's pins
- Cork board or piece of soft wood
- Paper and coloured pencils (optional)
- Iron and pressing cloth

PREVENT FRAYING **Tip**
To prevent the ribbons fraying while you handle them, apply a little clear nail varnish or fray check to each end and leave to dry before you begin weaving. Alternatively, wrap a thin strip of sticky tape around the ribbon at each cutting point and then snip through the ribbon and tape so there is tape left on each cut end. Do not remove the sticky tape until you have finished making the cushion.

1 Planning the design Decide how you wish to arrange the ribbons. You may find it helpful to start with a colour sketch or to arrange a few ribbons before you start. Alternatively, you can take pot luck and see what pattern emerges as you place the ribbons. Provided the ribbon colours all go well together, there is no reason why a random arrangement shouldn't work.

2 Preparing the interfacing Pin the interfacing to the cork or piece of soft wood with the adhesive side facing up. Place the pins as close to the edge as possible where they will be out of the way. Turn the board so the short edges of the interfacing are at the sides.

3 Arranging the vertical ribbons Starting at one short edge, lay the 28cm (11in) long strips of ribbon vertically over the interfacing, so their edges butt together. Follow your sketch or test arrangement, or decide on the order as you go along.

▲ *Woven silk ribbons create a luxurious cushion front. If you can't find ribbons in colours you want, make them from fabric strips. Press the edges under to neaten, using a binder maker for speed.*

5 Arranging the horizontal ribbons Lay the longer strips of ribbon out next to the pinned ribbons and at right angles to them. Decide if you are happy with their order and rearrange them as necessary for a pleasing effect.

4 Pinning the vertical ribbons Rearrange the ribbons as necessary until you are happy with their order, then pin them in place at the top end only, angling the pins outwards. Make sure the ribbons are straight and parallel.

7 Weaving the next ribbons Weave the second ribbon through the vertical ribbons in the same way, this time taking it under and over the vertical ribbons. Pin it in place. Continue like this until all the ribbons are pinned in place. The lowest horizontal ribbon should be exactly in line with the bottom of the interfacing.

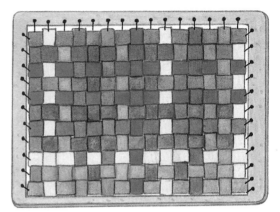

8 Bonding the ribbons Set your iron to a relatively cool temperature and gently press the woven ribbons between the pins, using a pressing cloth to protect the ribbons. When the ribbons have bonded to the interfacing, remove all the pins and press the ends of the ribbons to bond them in place too. Turn the ribbon fabric over and press again from the other side. Machine zigzag around the edge of the bonded ribbon fabric for added security.

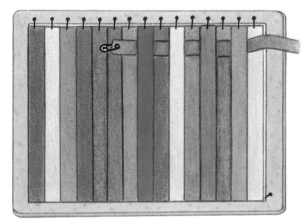

6 Weaving the first ribbon Fasten a safety pin to the end of the first ribbon and weave it over and under the vertical ribbons. Arrange the ribbon so it is parallel to the edges of the interfacing and positioned exactly in line with the top edge. Remove and replace pins as necessary. Remove the safety pin and then pin the ribbon to the interfacing at each end.

9 Embroidering the ribbons Thread the embroidery needle with two strands of cotton in any colour. Work a large cross-stitch across the woven edges where four ribbons meet. Work a vertical cross on top, in line with the edges of the ribbons to complete the star. Repeat at several other joining points. Switch to another colour of cotton and do the same thing. Keep changing colour and working the cross stitches until all the ribbons have been secured at their joining points.

10 Attaching the cushion back Pin the woven ribbons to the furnishing fabric with right sides facing. Stitch them together around the edges, taking a 1cm (⅜in) seam allowance and leaving a gap in one edge 10cm (4in) long to turn the cover out. Trim the seam allowances at the corners for ease, then turn the cover right sides out. Stuff the cushion with filling or insert a cushion pad, then slip stitch the opening to close it.

Weaving variations

The cushion on the previous page was made from ribbons woven together fairly randomly, but you can create some eye-catching results by limiting your colours and arranging them in a regular sequence. Here are some patterns you might like to try.

Patchwork squares

This pattern relies on using equal-width ribbons in three colours, with one light (**1**), one mid-tone (**2**) and one dark tone (**3**). Lay the ribbons in the same order vertically and horizontally.

1 Preparing the vertical ribbons Pin a row of 17 ribbons to iron-on interfacing, following the sequence **1, 2, 1, 3, 1, 2, 1, 3** and so on, ending with ribbon **1**. You can use more or fewer ribbons, but you must add or deduct them in lots of four to maintain the sequence.

2 Weaving the pattern Weave the horizontal ribbons through the vertical ones in the same order (**1, 2, 1, 3**) but in the following way. Weave ribbon **1** under one ribbon, then weave it over two, under two, over two, under two to the end. Weave ribbon **2** under one ribbon, over one, under one and so on to the end. Weave the third ribbon – colour **1** – over two ribbons, under two, over two, under two and so on, then over the last ribbon. Next weave ribbon **3** over one ribbon, then under one, over three, under one, over three to the end. Repeat the four-row sequence until you complete the weaving.

Zigzag weave

This pattern is created using ribbons in just two colours, **1** and **2**. The two ribbons can be of different widths, if required. Use an odd number of ribbons to create the design.

1 Preparing the vertical ribbons Pin an odd number of ribbons in vertical rows to iron-on interfacing, alternating colours **1** and **2**.

2 Weaving the horizontal ribbons Weave ribbon **1** over two ribbons, under two, over two, under two to the end. Next weave ribbon **2** under one, then in the sequence over two, under two, over two, under two to the end. Switch back to ribbon **1** and weave under two ribbons, over two, under two, over two to the end. Finally, use ribbon **2** to weave over one, then in the sequence under two, over two, under two, over two to the end. Repeat this four-row sequence until you complete the weaving.

Basket weave

This is a very simple pattern which uses wide satin ribbons in two colours for the basic pattern, with a narrower jacquard ribbon added to alternate horizontal rows. You can use any number of ribbons in each direction.

Weaving the ribbons Pin the two satin ribbons alternately to the iron-on interfacing in vertical rows. Weave the horizontal ribbons under and over them in the same way as the cushion on the previous page, but centre a narrow jacquard ribbon over the top of alternate ribbons.

patchwork squares

zigzag weave

basket weave

Appliqué patchwork cushion

*Combine three different needlecraft skills – appliqué,
embroidery and patchwork – to create a colourful country-style
cushion with an autumn apple theme.*

Using a range of different sewing skills in one project can create really eye-catching effects, and it brings variety to your work, too. In this cushion cover, all the colours and patterns in the patchwork squares, appliquéd apples and the blanket stitch are cleverly coordinated to produce a charming finished effect.

The apple motifs are fused to the square patches with a bonding fabric, and edged with blanket stitch for added decoration and strength. The patches are then stitched together and framed by a neat mitred border.

Patchwork is most appealing when it looks as though the different fabrics have been put together at random. In fact, this effortless look takes some careful thinking. The secret is to limit the colours you use. The colour scheme of this cushion, for example, is dominated by the border, which is made of checked Madras cotton. The other elements – the

▲ *A clever mix of three simple sewing techniques makes a delightful cushion cover. Use fabrics in glowing autumn colours to add warmth to your room.*

patchwork fabrics, the bold print used for the apple motifs, and the stranded embroidery threads chosen for the stitched edging round the appliqué – echo the border's palette of warm harvest colours. The final result is a pleasingly coordinated, colourful look.

Making the cushion

Choose a mixture of checked and striped fabrics for the square patches, borders and back. For the appliquéd apple motifs, cotton furnishing fabrics with bold designs work well against the stripes and checks. Make sure that all the fabrics are firmly woven, colourfast and preshrunk. The finished cushion cover measures 43cm (17in) square.

You will need

♦ **Pieces of four different checked and striped cotton fabrics for the patchwork**

♦ **Printed cotton furnishing fabric with flowers, fruit and leaves for the apple motifs**

♦ **70cm (³⁄₄yd) checked Madras cotton fabric, 90cm (36in) wide for border and back**

♦ **Tracing paper and thin card**

♦ **Water-soluble pen**

♦ **Bondaweb**

♦ **Crewel needle, size 7**

♦ **Stranded embroidery cotton in green, plus one other colour to tone with printed fabric**

♦ **Cushion pad**

1 Making the templates Trace the apple, stalk and leaf outlines from the full size template, right. Transfer on to thin card and cut out.

2 Preparing the apple motifs Decide which areas of the printed fabric to use for the apples. Lay the apple template on chosen area and draw round it with a water-soluble pen. Cut out, leaving a generous margin all round. Repeat to make nine apples. Prepare the motifs following the directions on page 61. Remove pen marks.

3 Preparing the leaves and stalks Prepare the stalks and leaves in the same way as the apple motifs, using the green areas of the fabric.

4 Applying the motifs Cut nine 12cm (4³⁄₄in) squares from a mixture of the striped and checked fabrics. Lay the squares out, arranging the stripes horizontally as well as vertically. Place an apple and stalk and one or two leaf motifs on each patch. See page 61 for directions on fusing the motifs in place.

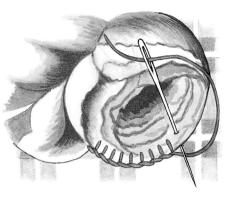

5 Adding the embroidery Using all six threads of stranded embroidery cotton and the crewel needle, work blanket stitch all round each motif. Use green for the leaves and stalks and the toning colour for the apples.

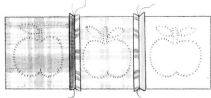

6 Joining the patches Lay out the appliquéd squares in their correct positions. Then, taking a 1cm (³⁄₈in) seam allowance, stitch the squares together neatly in rows of three. Press the seams open. Stitch the three rows together to form a square, making sure that the seams match. Press seams open.

7 Preparing the border Cut four strips of fabric 47 x 8.5cm (18½ x 3¼in). Following steps **3–4** on page 54, prepare and join the border strips.

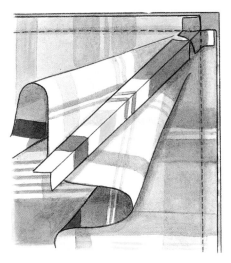

8 Attaching the border With right sides together, pin inner edges of border to outer edge of patchwork. Stitch in place, taking a 1cm (³⁄₈in) seam allowance. Clip the border seam allowances just below the stitching line and press the border flat.

9 Finishing the cushion Cut two pieces of fabric 45 x 27cm (17¾ x 10⅝in) for the cushion cover back. Attach the back panels to the front to complete the cushion cover, as in step **6** on page 54. Insert the cushion pad.

apple, leaf and stalk templates for tracing

Appliqué

Appliqué is stitching fabric shapes on to a background fabric to create designs. You can stitch the shapes by hand or machine, or you can fuse them on with a bonding fabric. It is a versatile technique that can be used to decorate many items from clothing to soft furnishings.

Materials

Fabric The easiest form of appliqué uses motifs cut from printed fabrics. Look out for motifs with bold, smooth outlines, as these are the easiest to cut neatly. Most firm, colourfast fabrics can be used, but they should have the same care properties as the main fabric to make laundering easier. Avoid stretchy or loosely woven fabrics.

Another option is to cut your appliqué shapes from patterned or plain fabrics using a template. Firmly-woven, smooth fabrics are best for this type of appliqué too.

Alternatively, non-woven fabrics, such as leather, felt, net and PVC, make good appliqué motifs because they don't fray. As they don't have a grain, they are easier to cut out.

Bonding fabric, such as Bondaweb, is really useful for appliqué. It can be used to fuse the appliqué motif to the main fabric, and will help to reinforce the motif at the same time.

Scissors must be sharp. Use dressmaking scissors to cut the fabric pieces out roughly, and small scissors to cut out fine details.

Needles and pins. Use fine, sharp pins and needles which will pierce the fabric without snagging or making large holes.

Thread should be matched to the colour of the appliqué motif.

Dressmakers' marker pen to draw the design outlines on to your background fabric.

Frame (optional). An embroidery or quilting frame helps to hold the fabric taut when stitching appliqué motifs in place by hand.

Paper. Graph paper, tracing paper and thin card are useful if you plan to do your own appliqué designs.

Bonded machine appliqué

This is the easiest and quickest appliqué technique, making it ideal for beginners. For the appliqué you can either use motifs from patterned fabric, as shown above, or cut out bold shapes from plain fabric. If you are using patterned fabric, look for motifs with smooth outlines, as these are the easiest to sew.

The appliqué motifs are first fused to the fabric with a bonding fabric, such as *Bondaweb*. This not only holds the motif in place, so that it doesn't slip while you are stitching it, but it also strengthens and stiffens the motif, creating a smoother finish.

To prevent fraying and to make sure the motifs are firmly attached, the edge of the motif is neatened with close machine zigzag. Fabrics that do not fray, such as felt or net, do not need a zigzag finish. However, since the bonding fabric may come loose with laundering, it's best to secure the motif, either with machine straight stitches or hand slipstitch.

1 Preparing the motif Cut out a piece of bonding fabric slightly larger than the motif. Following the manufacturer's instructions, place the bonding fabric rough side down on the wrong side of the fabric; press with a medium hot iron to bond the materials together.

2 Cutting out the motif Cut out motifs with the right side of the fabric uppermost, using small, sharp scissors for detailed shapes.

3 Attaching the motif Peel off the backing paper and position the motif on the background fabric. Cover it with a damp cloth and press with a medium hot iron. Leave the fabric to cool.

4 Zigzag stitching With an open zigzag, stitch around the appliqué shape, covering the raw edges. With a close zigzag, stitch around the shape again. Pull the threads through to the back of the work and fasten them off.

DECORATIVE EMBROIDERY

For a bold decorative finish, you can stitch round the outer edges of an appliqué motif with a hand embroidery stitch, such as closely worked blanket stitch, instead of machine zigzag stitch. This is a particularly good option if your sewing machine doesn't do a neat zigzag stitch. Work the stitches close together to cover the raw edges of the fabric.

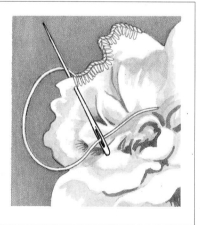

Hand appliqué

2 **Preparing the motif** Stitch round the appliqué shape just outside the seamline with tiny running stitches. This will reinforce the shape and help to prevent it fraying while you are stitching it on.

5 **Attaching the motif** Place the prepared shape on to the background fabric in the required position. Tack the motif in place with diagonal stitches across the centre of the motif. This will ensure that the motif is really flat and smooth.

Using a thread which matches the colour of the motif, slipstich all round the motif, taking tiny stitches.

Hand appliqué produces a softer, slightly puffier look than machine appliqué, and it has a distinctly hand-made look which makes it ideal for heirloom items, such as quilts.

If required, the softness of the appliqué can be emphasized by adding a layer of lightweight wadding under the shape. Alternatively, you can give the appliqué a crisp look by applying lightweight iron-on interfacing. If you are working on a patterned background fabric, interfacing will also help to prevent the pattern showing through pale motifs.

When working appliqué by hand, a narrow seam allowance around the shape is tucked under before the shape is slipstitched in place on the background fabric. The process is a bit more time-consuming than the machine method, but it is usually neater when working with small or fiddly shapes.

3 **Triming the fabric** Trim the fabric along the inner marked line. Cut small notches to the stitched line on outer curves, and snip to the stitched line along inner curves. Clip across any outer corners and snip to the stitched line on any inside corners for ease.

FAST HAND APPLIQUE

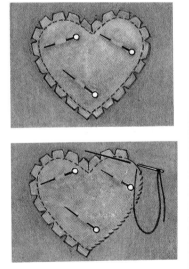

For quick appliqué, prepare your motif as in steps 1-3 for *Hand Appliqué*. Without turning the raw edges under, pin the motif in place on your background fabric. Slipstitch round the motif, tucking under the raw edges with the point of your needle as you sew. Take care to ensure a smooth, regular outline round the motif.

1 **Cutting out the motif** Working from the right side of the fabric, mark a 3mm (⅛in) seam allowance all round the motif, using a dressmakers' pencil. Roughly cut the shape out just beyond this line.

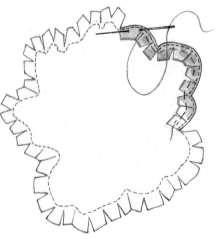

4 **Tacking down the edges** Turn under the raw edges of the motif so that the stitched line is just out of view. Finger press the edges, then tack them down.

Patchwork delights

*Whenever you use it in your home, patchwork adds
texture and eye-catching detail, enriching the decor with its
variations of pattern, shape and colour.*

Originally, patchwork was devised as a cost-cutting way of recycling old clothes to make warm bed covers. Today it is appreciated as much for its decorative value as its practical advantages.

Patchwork furnishings are highly adaptable and add colour, pattern and texture to any room scheme – they are just as effective in adding warmth and focus to a streamlined contemporary look as they are in emphasizing the cosy informality of a country-cottage setting.

Patchwork also fits naturally into any room in the house. It's an enduring classic in the bedroom, often pressed into service as a casual throw over a sofa or cushion cover for the living room, and works just as well as a cheerful accessory in the kitchen or bathroom.

▲ *Block booking These covers, based on traditional patchwork patterns, help to coordinate all the patterns and colours in this pretty room. The design on the righthand cushion is known as Pinwheel and can be recognized by the distinctive wheel at the centre. On the left, the Basket is first patched together, then stitched on to the cover itself.*

The craft of patchwork

Patchwork is the joining together of shaped pieces (patches) of patterned or coloured fabrics to form a cloth mosaic. Traditionally, it was created by hand, in blocks (manageable sections of several individual shaped pieces) but fortunately even most of the classic designs can now easily and more speedily be stitched on a machine.

The pattern-making possibilities are almost infinite, although the classic patterns – one-patch designs based on a single geometric shape such as a triangle, square or hexagon – are still the most popular.

You can also try out your own patchwork ideas using left-over scraps of furnishing or dressmaking fabrics. Use either commercially available template shapes or cut out your own from stiff card. If you do create your own design, sketch out and fit your ideas on a piece of paper first, or arrange your scraps in the way you want to use them, so that you can make sure that the patterns and colours balance properly.

▶ *Adapt to fit* Made from a stylish selection of different checks, this lovable bear definitely falls into the 'patched' category. To recreate his charming look, adapt a standard bear pattern by using different fabrics for each panel.

▲ *Bed of roses* If the thought of working with small patches to create a large item is daunting, increase the scale. This quilt is made of large but manageable blocks of fabric which have been quilted and then sewn together, yet it retains the charm of traditional patchwork.

◀ *Combining crafts* Patchwork within patchwork can create interesting patterns. The central coloured sections of this covetable quilt are made individually by pieced, block patchwork then set into a large pattern of white and green panels. Together they create an eye-catching throw which gives a new lease of life to this sofa.

▼ **Heart to heart** *Patchwork pieces can be virtually any shape you want. Here heart-shaped patches are appliquéd to squares of plain calico, which are then stitched together and quilted to form the centre panel of a country-style wall-hanging.*

▶ **Treasure trove**
Acquiring patchwork quilts can become just as much a passion as making them. This collection of neatly folded colourful quilts would look just as good on open display shelves as it does here; and it could add colour and warmth to a traditional bathroom as well as provide interest in this bedroom storage area.

▶*Applied patchwork* The crafts of patchwork, quilting and appliqué are often used together to create a special effect. Here, the three crafts combine to make a teddy bear quilt with real child appeal.

▼*Creative display* Thrown over an occasional table, this star-studded patchwork quilt turns a plain corner of the living room into an interesting focal point. If you use a treasured quilt in this way, protect it with a lacy top cloth or easy-to-clean glass.

▶*Jigsaw puzzles* One of the great pleasures of patchwork comes from the numerous ways you can arrange patches of the same shapes, colour and pattern to create different designs.

Patchwork

Patchwork is the stitching together of fabric shapes to form a larger unit, which can be anything from a pin cushion to a bed quilt. It's a practical and attractive way to use up fabric scraps and remnants, and offers plenty of scope for creativity.

There are two main types of patchwork: one-shape patchwork, in which all the pieces are exactly the same shape and size, and block unit patchwork, where differently shaped and sized pieces are stitched together to form basic blocks; the blocks are then joined together to form a whole.

Materials

Fabrics of all kinds can be used for patchwork, but choose fabrics that are suitable for the article you're making. Mediumweight, evenly woven cotton is the easiest to use, but you can mix fabric types, provided they are compatible in weight, construction and laundering requirements. Natural fibres are best – synthetic fabrics don't hold a crease well. Choose a mixture of plain and printed fabrics to create an interesting design. Wash the fabric gently before use, to remove any manufacturer's finish and loose dye, and to pre-shrink it.

Drawing materials are necessary to design and chart a patchwork pattern. You'll need **pencils**, a **rubber**, a **ruler**, **colouring pencils** and **graph paper**. A **compass** and a **protractor** are required for drawing and dividing circles. **Scissors** and **fine card** are necessary for making templates.

Useful **sewing materials** for patchwork include a **dressmaker's marker pencil**, **scissors**, **pins**, **needles** – for either hand or machine sewing – and **matching sewing threads**.

Design options

A wide range of patchwork designs has evolved over the years, most of which are based on the square or the circle.

Squares and triangles

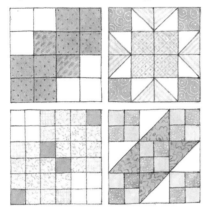

The most popular and easiest shape to use in patchwork is the square. It can be any size and may be divided into smaller squares within a grid system. The more squares in the grid, the greater the potential for design variations.

The introduction of diagonal lines, from one corner of the square or rectangle to the diagonally opposite corner, creates more diverse and intricate patterns as triangles are introduced. Using colour, the triangles may be grouped with other shapes to create unusual effects. Many interesting designs, like the ones shown above, can be produced simply by using squares, half-square triangles and quarter-square triangles.

Circles

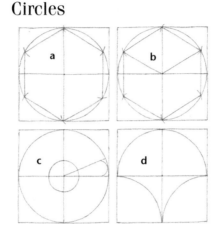

The circle can form the basis for many patchwork designs. Always draw it within a square, with the halfway lines marked in, as shown above, to help you plot your design. You can divide the circumference into six arcs and join the marks to form a hexagon (**a**). The hexagon can be divided into triangles or diamonds (**b**). You can draw concentric circles within the main circle, or divide the circle into wedges (**c**). The classic patchwork shell shape is produced from a semicircle and two quarter circles (**d**).

Dividers and borders

Dividers may be added between blocks of patchwork to give definition to each section. Use a border to frame your design or to extend it to the required size. Plan for any dividers and borders when you chart your design.

Using colour

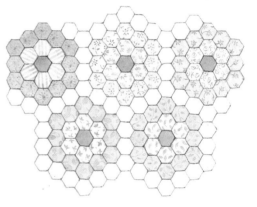

A basic understanding of colour is essential when you're planning a patchwork design. For the design to have maximum impact, you'll need to use dominant colours for areas you want to emphasize, such as the flower centres on a traditional grandmother's flower garden patchwork (shown above), and weaker colours for surrounding areas.

As a general rule, warm colours, such as red, yellow and orange are more dominant than cool colours, such as blue, green and purple. However, the strength of a colour is also effected by its tone and by the colours which surround it. Take time to experiment with different colour arrangements, and chart your whole design using coloured pencils as close in colour and tone to your fabrics as possible, so that you can judge the finished effect. If you are still unsure, make up a small sample of the patchwork design, using different fabrics and colours to see the effect they have on one another.

Patchwork preparation

Before you start stitching your patchwork, you'll need to plan the design, cut out templates, calculate fabric requirements, and cut out the fabric patches.

Charting the design

Plan your design on paper. Check the proportions of the design elements, give them measurements and check that they fit into the finished measurement of your piece of patchwork. Alter the size and number of units, if necessary, or add a border to bring it up to size. Draw each unit in your patchwork to finished size on graph paper – you will use these drawings to make your templates. Chart the design to scale on graph paper and colour it in to use as a stitching guide.

Making templates

Templates are used to cut out the fabric patches and, in hand-sewn patchwork, the backing papers. You'll need templates for every shape in your design. You can buy standard shapes in metal or plastic from craft suppliers, or make your own from card.

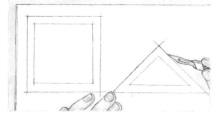

Trace the basic shapes from your finished size patchwork diagrams on to card. Cut them out to make the marking templates for the backing papers in hand-sewn patchwork. Lay these templates over card and draw around them. Add a 6mm (¼in) seam allowance all round and cut them out to make the cutting templates for the fabric patches.

Fabric requirements

Following your coloured design chart, count the number of shapes in each fabric and list them. Take the first cutting template and calculate how many times it can be repeated across the fabric width. Divide this figure into the number of shapes required in the fabric, then multiply the result by the depth of one shape. This will give you the total length of fabric needed for the shape. Repeat this procedure for each shape and each fabric. Buy a little extra of each fabric to allow for mistakes.

Cutting out the shapes

Lay the cutting template on the wrong side of the fabric, with one edge on the straight grain. With a dressmaker's pencil, mark around the template, working in rows across the fabric width until you have the required number of shapes. If you are using a one-way printed fabric, make sure you lay the template in the desired direction of the print.

One-shape patchwork

One-shape patchwork is made up of small patches of the same shape and size, in different prints and colours, often arranged to create a mosaic effect. It is traditionally hand-sewn, especially when the shapes are intricate, such as hexagons and shells. The patches are tacked over backing papers, pressed, then sewn together at the folded edges. The tacking is then unpicked and the papers removed.

Grandmother's garden

This one-shape patchwork design is based on a hexagon. The colours and prints are planned to create the impression of flowers – one fabric is used for the flower centre, with a contrasting fabric for the surrounding 'petals'. The flowers may be unified by using the same colour for every central hexagon. Each flower is sewn separately, then connected with 'paths' of plain hexagons to form a whole. Chart the design and cut out the templates before you begin.

You will need

◆ **Plain and patterned fabrics**

◆ **Hexagonal cutting and marking templates**

◆ **Paper for backing papers**

◆ **Scissors, pins and paper clips**

◆ **Matching sewing threads**

1 Preparing the patches Using the cutting template, mark up and cut out the fabric hexagons. Using the marking template, cut out the backing papers. Pin a backing paper centrally on to the wrong side of a patch. Fold the fabric edges over the paper, secure them with paper clips and tack them in place. Press the folded edges gently, with the tip of an iron. Repeat for all the patches.

2 Joining the patches With the right sides together, match the central hexagon of one flower to one of the adjoining 'petal' hexagons. Oversew the two together along one edge with tiny stitches. Open out the patches. Repeat with the other five petal hexagons.

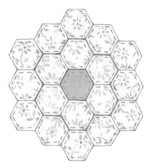

3 Forming the flowers With the right sides together, oversew the sides of all the petals together. Follow steps 2 and 3 to sew another row of petals around the first. Make up other patchwork flowers as necessary. Join the flowers together with 'paths' of plain hexagons, following your chart and oversewing the patches together as for the flowers.

4 Finishing the patchwork When all the patches have been stitched together, place the patchwork right side down on a padded surface, such as a table covered with towels. Smooth it to shape, then pin the edges in place through the padded surface. Remove the tacking threads and backing papers. Press the patchwork, using a damp cloth and moderate heat.

Block unit patchwork

Block unit patchwork evolved in America, where the pioneer women developed many evocatively named designs which are still popular today, such as Hunter's Star, Crossed Canoes and Log Cabin. The technique involves working square or rectangular sections or 'blocks' of the design individually, then sewing them together to create the finished item. Each block can carry the same design, or different ones.

Block unit patchwork is a simple way to work large projects, such as quilts. As each block is a manageable size, it's also ideal for working complex patchwork designs.

There are two types of block unit patchwork: pieced, in which patches are joined together edge-to-edge to form the blocks; and appliquéd, in which patches are stitched on to a base fabric. In both cases, the blocks are first joined together to form strips, then the strips are stitched together. You can work block unit patchwork by machine or by hand – or even both, by working the individual blocks by hand, then machine stitching them together to form a whole.

Missouri star (pieced)

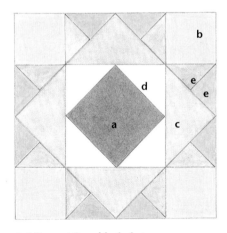

▲ *Missouri Star block design*

You will need

- ◆ **Patchwork fabrics**
- ◆ **Tracing paper, pencil and card**
- ◆ **Graph paper and colouring pencils**
- ◆ **Matching sewing threads**
- ◆ **Scissors and pins**

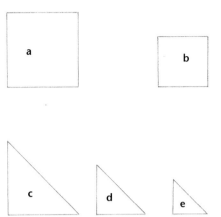

1 Preparing to sew Draw the Missouri Star block design to the desired size, then chart and colour it; use your chart as a colour guide throughout. Working from the finished drawing, make the necessary cutting templates to the correct size in card, then cut out your patches in fabric. For information on charting designs and cutting out templates and patches, see page 68.

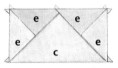

2 Stitching triangular units With the right sides together and the raw edges matching, stitch together pairs of small triangles (e) along one short edge. Open out the patches and press the seams open. With the right sides together, stitch the long edge of each pair of small triangles to the corresponding short edge of each large triangle (c). Press the seam allowances towards the small triangles.

3 The top and bottom strips With the right sides together, stitch a small square (b) to each short end of two of the triangular units. Press the seam allowances towards the squares.

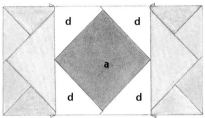

4 Forming the centre strip With the right sides together, stitch the long edge of one medium triangle (**d**) to each side of the large square (**a**). Press the seam allowances towards the triangles. With the right sides together, stitch the corresponding long edge of the two remaining triangular units to each end of the central unit. Press the seam allowances towards the adjacent side units.

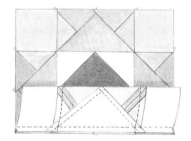

5 Joining the strips With the right sides facing, stitch the top and bottom strips to the central strip, making sure that you stitch right up to the points of the triangles. Press the seam allowances towards the outlying strips.

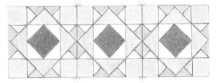

6 Completing the patchwork Stitch the other blocks in the same way, following steps 2-5. With the right sides facing, join the blocks together to form strips, inserting dividers if desired. Then join the strips together. Press and finish the patchwork as described on page 68.

Log cabin (appliquéd)

▲ *Log Cabin block design*
Strips of fabric are sewn to the base block around a central square. The strips are usually sewn on in a light and dark sequence, and the central square is generally red, to represent the fire in the hearth. Log cabin requires less preparation than many designs, because no templates are required – the strips are all the same width and very simple to cut out.

The instructions given here are for machine-stitched patchwork, but you can easily adapt them for hand-sewing. Take 6mm (¼in) seam allowances throughout.

You will need

- ◆ **Patchwork fabrics**
- ◆ **Firmly woven fabric for base**
- ◆ **Tracing paper, pencil and ruler**
- ◆ **Graph paper and colouring pencils**
- ◆ **Matching sewing threads**
- ◆ **Scissors and pins**

1 Preparing to sew Draw the Log cabin block design to the desired finished size, making the centre square twice the width of the surrounding strips. Chart and colour the design. Cut out the base blocks and centre squares to the same size as your drawing, plus 6mm (¼in) all round. For information on charting designs, see page 68.

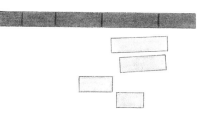

2 Cutting the strips Following the grain, cut or tear strips across your chosen fabric, to the width of the finished strips plus 12mm (½in). Measure the length of each strip on your diagram, then mark and cut the long strips to the required lengths, adding 12mm (½in).

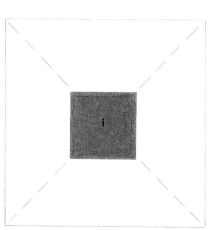

3 Starting the patchwork Tack diagonal lines across the base fabric block from the lower corners to the opposite top corners. Place the centre square (i) right side up, centrally on the fabric base block, matching the corners to the tacking lines, and tack it in place.

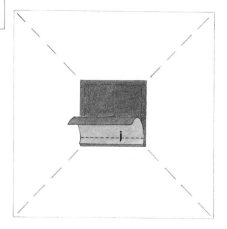

4 Adding the first strip With the right sides together and the edges matching, stitch the shortest strip (**j**) to the bottom edge of the centre square, stitching through the backing fabric at the same time. Press the strip to the right side.

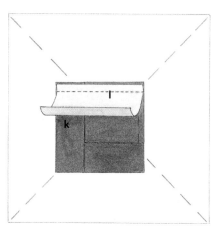

5 Adding strips With the right sides together, stitch the next longest strip (**k**) to the left edge of the centre square and the end of the first strip. Turn the strip to the right side and press it flat. Stitch the next strip (**l**) to the top edge of the centre square and the end of the previous strip. Press the strip to the right side. Continue stitching strips round the square in this way, working in a clockwise direction, until the block is complete.

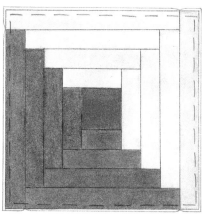

6 Completing the patchwork Tack the outlying strip edges to the base block, then finish the patchwork as for the *Missouri star*, step 6.

GROUPING SHAPES
If you are making a block unit patchwork featuring several different shapes and sizes, sew pieces of the same size, shape and colour on to a length of thread for safe keeping.

Hexagon patchwork

Try your hand at the craft of handstitched template patchwork with this summer-fresh gingham table cloth, trimmed with a border of hexagon rosettes.

Handstitched patchwork using templates, although time consuming, is a very pleasurable pastime. In the midst of today's hectic lifestyle, it provides a relaxing and satisfying hobby. If you have never previously attempted this kind of needlework, you will find traditional English hexagonal patchwork makes the perfect starting point.

Of the many shapes used in template patchwork, the six-sided hexagon is the simplest to use – the wide angles at the corners are easy to fold neatly and the hexagons fit together to create pretty designs with a floral look. Seven hexagons joined together make a single rosette; a double rosette can be formed by adding another border of hexagons. The traditional design known as 'Grandmother's Flower Garden' is made by linking double rosettes together with plain fabric hexagons to form a quilt – the rosettes represent the flowers and linking hexagons the garden path.

A large quilt is a time-consuming and daunting project for a beginner. For a taste of the art of template patchwork, try this gingham table cloth trimmed with an exuberant border of hexagon rosettes. It can be stitched in just a few hours and you can make matching napkins and place mats to complete the summery look.

▼ *Tea in the garden becomes a special occasion when the table is dressed with this pretty gingham patchwork cloth and matching hexagon rosette place mats.*

Materials and equipment

From your sewing box you will need a sharp dressmaker's chalk pencil for drawing round the template, sharp scissors for accurate cutting out, and fine pins. Use a fine needle and thread for stitching the hexagon patches together.

Fabric Lightweight pure cotton is ideal for template patchwork, and many fabric stores sell patchwork fabrics in a wide range of colours and prints. You can use remnants, but make sure before you start that they are colourfast and won't shrink, and use fabrics that are all the same weight.

Templates The pattern from which patches are cut is called a template. You can cut your own template from thick card, but bought templates are more accurate and durable. They are

made from hardwearing metal or plastic and generally consist of two sections. The outer 'window' frame is used for cutting the fabric patches and includes a 6mm (¼in) seam allowance, and the smaller solid shape is used for cutting the linings which support the patchwork as it is stitched.

Linings Paper for linings are removed when the patchwork is complete. The paper must be firm enough so that you can feel the edges inside the folded fabric. To save money, use stiff pages from discarded glossy magazines, old greeting cards, envelopes or notepaper. If the fabric is so fine that the turnings will show through, you can use lightweight iron-on interfacing instead of paper and leave it in the finished work.

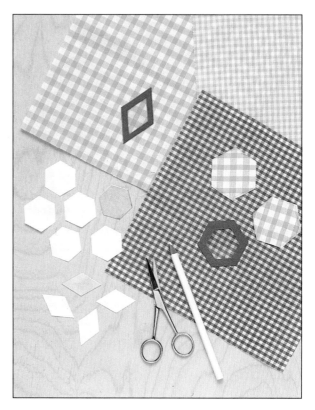

Making a hexagon rosette

A rosette is formed from seven hexagons – choose different fabrics for the centre hexagon and the 'petal' hexagons. Don't remove the tacking threads until the rosette has been joined to its background.

1 Cutting the linings Place the inner template on paper or iron-on interfacing and draw round with a sharp pencil. Cut out the linings accurately.

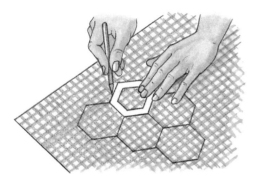

2 Cutting out the fabric hexagons Position the window template on the right side of the fabric. Line up the top and bottom edges on the straight grain of the fabric and draw round the template with a sharp dressmaker's chalk pencil. Cut out the required number of hexagon patches.

3 Making a hexagon patch Place a paper or interfacing lining on the wrong side of each fabric patch, making sure it is centred and on the straight grain. Anchor paper with a pin, or fuse interfacing to fabric according to manufacturer's instructions. Fold fabric over lining on each side in turn and tack, making sure the corners are folded neatly.

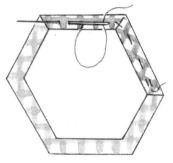

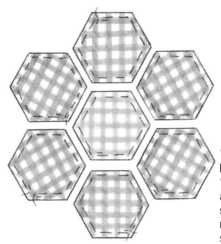

4 Joining the hexagons Lay out seven hexagons to form a rosette. Place the central hexagon and one 'petal' right sides together and join along one edge with tiny oversewing stitches. Open out the patches and repeat with the five remaining petals, so that each is stitched to the central hexagon and then stitched to its neighbours. Press the seams open.

You will need

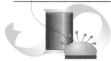

- 1.2m (1³⁄₈yd) green gingham with 6mm (¹⁄₄in) checks
- 50cm (⁵⁄₈yd) pink, mauve and turquoise gingham with 6mm (¹⁄₄in) checks
- 20cm (¹⁄₄yd) yellow gingham with 3mm (¹⁄₈in) checks
- 1m (1¹⁄₈yd) lightweight iron-on interfacing (Vilene)
- 3.75cm (1¹⁄₂in) hexagon template set
- 3.75cm (1¹⁄₂in) diamond template set
- White tacking and sewing threads
- Dressmaker's pencil
- Fine sewing needle and pins

▼ *You can easily make these napkins to match your table cloth. Cut a 43cm (17in) square of gingham for each napkin, and stitch a 6mm (¹⁄₄in) double hem all round. Following Making a hexagon rosette, steps 1-4, make up one rosette for each napkin and topstitch it in one corner. Remove tacking thread.*

Making the table cloth

The finished table cloth measures 125cm (49¹⁄₂in) square. The hexagon rosettes are linked by diamond-shaped patches to form four border strips, which are stitched to each side of the table cloth. The cloth is made from lightweight gingham. To prevent the background fabric and turnings showing through, use lightweight iron-on interfacing for the linings. The fabric quantities given below are for fabric 115cm (45in) wide. If you would like to make matching napkins you can use leftover gingham for the rosettes, but you will need to buy some extra green gingham for the napkins.

1 Making the table cloth From the green gingham, cut a 101.5cm (40in) square. Turn in, press and machine stitch a 6mm (¹⁄₄in) double hem all round.

2 Making the rosettes Following *Making a hexagon rosette*, steps 1-4, make eight pink, six blue and six mauve rosettes, all with yellow gingham centres.

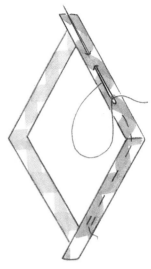

3 Making the diamond patches Using the diamond template and following *Making a hexagon rosette*, steps 1-3, cut out and make up 16 diamond patches in green gingham.

4 Planning the border strips Lay the table cloth out and place five rosettes along each edge. Alternate the colours and make sure that two rosettes of the same colour are not next to each other at the corners.

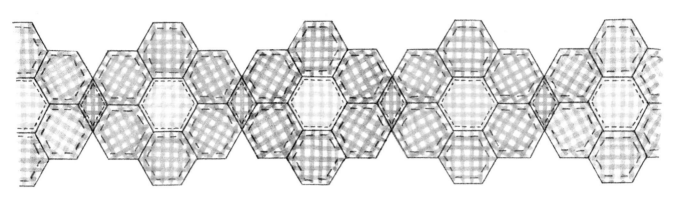

5 Finishing the border strips Use four diamond patches to join each set of five rosettes, stitching hexagons and diamonds together in the usual way to give four separate border strips. Then topstitch the yellow centre hexagons and the diamonds 3mm (⅛in) inside the seamline.

6 Attaching the borders to the cloth Pin the border strips to the cloth so that the top of the yellow centre is level with the edge of the table cloth hem, and the tip of the end hexagons are 2cm (¾in) in from the corners of the cloth. Topstitch all round the edge of each rosette 3mm (⅛in) in from the folded edges of the hexagons. Remove all tacking.

Making a place mat

To complement your patchwork table cloth, why not make a set of matching quilted hexagon place mats? Follow *Making a hexagon rosette*, steps 1-3, but fold and tack turnings on three sides only of the the petal patches. Join the hexagons following step 4, leaving the seam allowances on the outer edges unstitched; press. Place the rosette and a 23cm (9in) square of green gingham right sides together on top of a square of polyester wadding the same size. Pin and stitch round the rosette with a 6mm(¼in) seam allowance, leaving two adjacent sides open. Trim the wadding and green gingham, clip the corners, then turn through to the right side. Slipstitch the opening closed. Machine quilt round the centre hexagon and between the petals using invisible nylon thread as the top thread, following the 'stitch-in-the-ditch' method.

Hand stitches

Tacking stitch

This stitch is used to hold two or more layers of fabric in position temporarily while you work permanent stitches by hand or machine. Use a contrasting colour thread for your tacking stitches so that they are easy to see when you are removing them.

Working from right to left, pass the needle in and out of the fabric layers, making each stitch 6-10mm (¼-⅜in) long.

Flat hemming stitch

This is used to secure hems and other folded fabric edges on light and mediumweight fabrics.

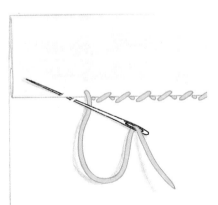

Working from right to left with the hem facing away from you, pick up a thread of the single fabric, then a thread of the fold and pull the needle through. Take care not to tighten the thread too much or the fabric will pucker.

Hemming slipstitch

This stitch is used to secure hems and other folded edges. It is hardly noticeable on the right side, making it ideal for fine and lightweight fabrics, and for stitching on decorative trims and patch pockets.

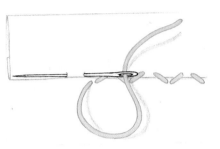

Work from right to left with the hem facing away from you. Pick up a thread of the single fabric, then slip the needle inside the hem fold.

Slipstitch

This is used to join two folded fabric edges together, such as an opening on a cushion cover. The stitches are almost invisible, giving a neat seam, and are worked from the right side of the fabric.

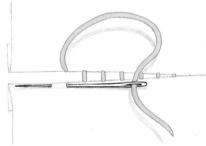

Place the two folded edges together with right sides facing you. Slip the needle inside the fold of one edge, then take the needle horizontally across to the other edge and slip it along that fold. Pull the thread to draw the edges together.

Tailors' tacks

Use tailors' tacks to transfer symbols from a paper pattern on to double layers of fabric. Pin the pattern in position on your fabric and don't remove the pattern until you have transferred all the pattern symbols with this stitch.

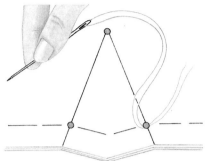

1 Starting the stitch With the point of a needle, make a small slit in the pattern across the symbols you wish to transfer. Take a small stitch through both layers of fabric with a double thread, leaving an unknotted end at least 8cm (3in) long.

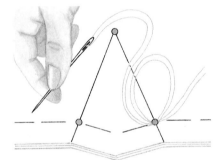

2 Completing the stitch Make a second stitch in the same place, leaving a 4cm (1½in) loop. Cut the thread, leaving an 8cm (3in) end.

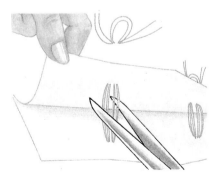

3 Removing the pattern When you have marked all the symbols, remove the paper pattern, taking care not to pull out the threads. Separate the layers of fabric and cut the thread between the two layers.

Blanket stitch

This is a decorative stitch used to neaten raw edges, especially along flat seams or edges.

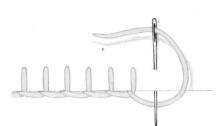

Work from left to right along the fabric edge, passing the needle through the fabric and over the working thread. Space the stitches evenly.

Ladder stitch

Use ladder stitch when joining two pieces of patterned fabric to make sure that the pattern matches exactly. Use large stitches for temporary tacking, and small stitches for the final stitch.

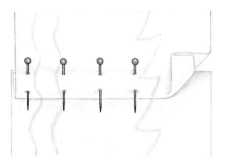

1 Preparing the fabric edges Press the seam allowance to the wrong side on one piece of fabric. Lap the folded edge over the other edge so the pattern matches. Pin the fabrics in place.

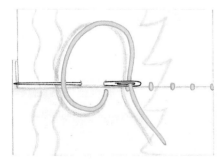

2 Stitching the fabric Slip the needle along the fold of the top layer, then take a small stitch through the bottom fabric close to the fold. If you are using the stitch as a tacking stitch, open out the fold before machine stitching the seam.

Buttonhole stitch

This is identical to blanket stitch (see left), but the stitches are placed close together for a very firm and strong finish. Use buttonhole stitch to neaten eyelets and buttonholes and to make bar tacks and belt loops.

You can use buttonhole stitch to work buttonholes, but tailors' buttonhole stitch, which has an extra twist, is more hardwearing.

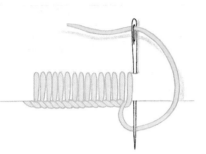

Work buttonhole stitch in exactly the same way as blanket stitch (see top left) but place the upright stitches close together.

Prick stitch

Prick stitch is a tiny backstitch which is worked from the right side to insert zips in fine fabric. You can also use it to secure several layers of fine fabric where machine stitching would cause the fabric to move and make an unsightly ridge.

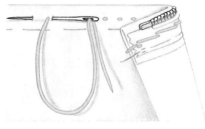

Working from right to left, take tiny stitches over one or two threads on the right side, and longer stitches on the wrong side.

Tailors' buttonhole

Use this stitch for buttonholes – it's more difficult to work than ordinary buttonhole stitch (left) but its knotted edge is more durable.

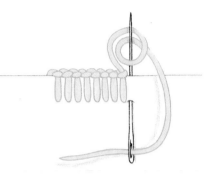

1 Making the basic stitch Work from left to right with the raw fabric edge facing away from you. Take a stitch upwards through the fabric, looping the thread around the needle.

2 Finishing the stitch Gently pull the thread to tighten the knot. Work the stitches close together so that the knots are touching.

Oversewing

Use this stitch when you want to neaten raw edges by hand.

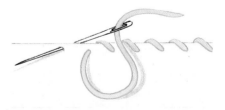

Hold the fabric with the raw edge facing away from you and work the stitches diagonally over the edge from right to left. Don't pull the thread too tight or the fabric will form a ridge.

Pattern quilting

*Machine quilting is a simple way to highlight the principal motifs
of a patterned fabric and add attractive surface texture to a whole variety of
projects, from wall hangings to place mats and shopping bags.*

The traditional technique of quilting ranges from purely decorative effects to smart and practical ways of adding warmth to clothing and furnishings.

Quilting involves stitching together three layers of fabric: a top layer – often a printed fabric, a middle, insulating layer of wadding to create the thickness,

and a backing fabric. Stitching through the thickness of all three layers creates the attractive texture of quilting.

The basic technique of quilting by machine or by hand is the same. However, machine quilting is quicker and the stitches are firmer, producing a stronger fabric that can withstand laundering or heavy wear and tear.

▲ *This set of colourful table mats makes an ideal first time quilting project. Instead of having to transfer a design to the fabric, you simply machine quilt round the large, clear motifs on a printed fabric. The edges are bound in a toning fabric for a neat finish.*

Materials and equipment

Top fabric (1) Choose a printed fabric with a design that has bold, simple outlines which you can machine stitch round easily. Firm, plain weave cottons in a medium weight are ideal. Avoid slippery fabrics for a first project as they are more difficult to sew. For placemats it is also important that all the fabrics, including the wadding, are washable and colourfast. Always allow a little extra fabric as the stitching tends to pull in the fabrics slightly, reducing the dimensions of the finished work.

Wadding (2) For machine quilting, the wadding should not be too thick – or you'll have difficulty feeding all the layers under the machine foot. Light or medIumweight polyester *wadding* is ideal, as it is washable and gives bulk without

weight. Interlining, such as *bump* or *domette*, is suitable as well but does not give the same depth of texture to the quilting once it is stitched.

Backing fabric (3) The wadding does not feed easily through the machine by itself, so it needs to be backed with fabric. If the quilting is to have a separate, unquilted lining, you can use a fine cotton or muslin as the backing fabric. When the backing serves as a visible, quilted lining as well, choose a fabric to match or contrast with the top fabric.

Thread Cotton-coated polyester thread is suitable for most fabrics. Choose a colour to match the predominant colour of the printed design.

Sewing machine settings

A standard sewing machine with a multi-purpose foot is fine for basic machine quilting. However, you can fit many modern machines with special attachments to make quilting easier. For example, an even-feed foot helps all

▲ *The top of this mat is quilted in the same way as the bound-edge design but, instead of binding the edges, it is lined. The lining is stitched to the top with right sides together, leaving a small gap through which to turn the mat the right way out. The mat is then topstitched all round the edge to stop the lining rolling to the front.*

the fabric layers move under the foot evenly, to prevent the fabric puckering as you stitch. A roller foot attachment produces similar results.

If your machine has an adjustable speed, this should be set to its slowest when you are quilting in order to give maximum control.

Stitch length

The stitch length depends largely on the thickness of the fabric being quilted, but a medium-length stitch is generally suitable. Use a No.14 (90) needle for the best results.

Quilting the fabric

It isn't necessary to quilt round all the motifs of the design; you can achieve very effective results by highlighting small areas of the pattern. When quilting round individual motifs, it's a good idea to practise your technique on a spare piece of fabric.

As a general rule, and especially if you are working parallel lines of quilting, start at the centre of the piece of work and stitch outwards in each direction. This helps to prevent the fabric from puckering as you stitch.

1 Preparing the fabrics Iron the top and backing fabrics to remove any creases. Place the backing fabric right side down on a flat surface and lay the wadding over it. Place the top layer of fabric, right side up, carefully over the wadding.

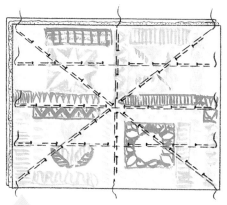

2 Securing the layers Using long fine pins, pin through all three layers, working from the centre outwards to the edge of the fabric. Tack the layers together following the pinned lines.

3 Quilting individual motifs Working from the right side, stitch round the main motifs of the pattern. Work those motifs closest to the centre first. Machine slowly with small straight stitches.

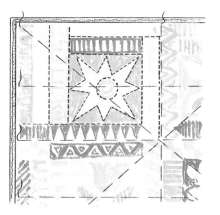

4 Neatening the thread ends Pull the top thread through to the wrong side of the work. Use a needle to stitch the thread ends back into the wadding. Simply cut off any threads around the edges of the fabric.

Tip

LARGE PROJECTS
For large pieces of work, secure the layers in two stages, tacking the wadding to the bottom fabric layer before attaching the top layer. This ensures that all the layers lie absolutely flat.

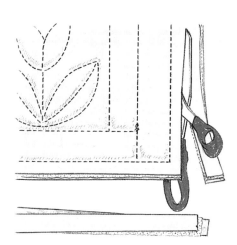

5 Completing the quilting When the quilting is complete and the thread ends secured, trim the quilted fabric to remove any excess wadding and neaten slightly distorted edges. Remove all the tacking threads. The quilted fabric is now ready to be made up as required.

▼ *After practising your quilting technique on a sample square of fabric, wadding and lining sandwiched together, you can put your test pieces to good use by turning them into handy pot holders.*

Bound-edge placemats

This version of the placemat is neatened with a bound edge, so a separate lining is not required. Use a ready-made bias binding, available from haberdashery departments – 2.5cm (1in) wide binding is ideal.

Each placemat measures approximately 40 x 32cm (15¾ x 12½in). However, the exact size depends on the actual fabric design you have chosen. For instance you may want to increase the size slightly to take in complete motifs. The fabric quantities given here are for four mats; double them if you want to make eight.

Study your fabric and decide which areas to quilt. You may want to emphasize the main outlines of the motifs or quilt the fabric in more detail.

You will need

For four mats in one pattern:

- ◆ 1m (1⅛yd) cotton print fabric
- ◆ 1m (1⅛yd) plain cotton fabric for backing
- ◆ 1m (1⅛yd) 100g (4oz) washable polyester wadding
- ◆ 2.5cm (1in) wide bias binding
- ◆ Matching thread
- ◆ Long fine pins
- ◆ Needle and tacking thread

▲ *With the edges neatened in a matching bias binding, the bound-edge placemats are reversible. The stitching pattern of the quilting is clearly visible on the coordinating backing fabric that also doubles as a lining.*

1 Cutting out the printed fabric Cut out a 45 x 37cm (17¾ x 14½in) rectangle for each placemat, taking care to centre any main motifs or position them in an attractive way. The measurements given allow for a seam allowance and ease taken up during quilting.

2 Cutting out wadding and backing Using the printed rectangle as a pattern, cut a piece of backing fabric and wadding to the same size. Repeat for each mat.

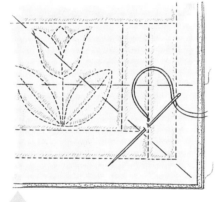

3 Quilting the design Following *steps 1-2, Quilting the fabric* on the previous page, pin and tack the three layers together. Machine quilt the chosen parts of the design, following *step 3*. Trim the quilted fabric to 42 x 34cm (16½ x 13½in) or to the desired size, depending on your print. This allows for a 1.2cm (½in) seam allowance round the edge.

4 Attaching the binding Measure round the edge of mat, add 4cm (1½in), and cut a strip of bias binding to this length. Attach the binding to the placemat following the instructions on pages 77-78, remembering to clip into the seam allowance to ease the bias binding round the corners smoothly.

Machine quilting large projects

You'll find it much quicker to quilt large items by machine than by hand. The stitches are also stronger, so items which will have a lot of wear, such as bedcovers, will last well.

Choose simple, geometric designs, with straight lines or large, open curves – it's difficult to stitch intricate curves by machine, especially when you are working with a lot of fabric.

Materials & equipment

Wadding Avoid very thick wadding, especially for large projects, as it makes the fabric too thick to fit under the sewing machine foot, and it will make large items too bulky and heavy to handle easily. The wadding should generally be at least 5-10cm (2-4in) larger all round than the top fabric. If you need to join pieces together, butt the edges and whipstitch them (see below).

Backing fabric It's best to choose a backing fabric with the same care properties as the main fabric. Pure cotton is easy to stitch and doesn't pucker as much as polyester-cotton blends. Sheeting is a good choice for large projects as it is available in wide widths which should not need to be joined. Like the wadding, it should generally be at least 5-10cm (2-4in) larger all round than the top fabric. If you need to join pieces, stitch them together with a standard seam.

Quilting bar This is attached to the machine foot to provide a guide for stitching parallel lines.

Twin needle This is useful for decorative stitching. You can thread it with two colours of thread for added decoration.

Sharp No 14 (90) needle This is suitable for most projects, but you may need a thicker or thinner needle for heavy or lightweight fabrics.

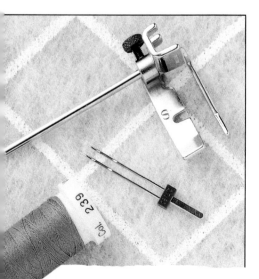

Quick marking aids

Iron-on backing For projects that don't need much padding, use a layer of iron-on quilted backing (Quiltex) to mark the quilting lines. This is lightly padded and it should be fused to the wrong side of the fabric like iron-on interfacing. Stitch along the outlines.

Masking tape A quick-and-easy way of marking out straight stitching lines on the fabric is to use masking tape. Position the tape on the fabric so that one edge marks the quilting line and then stitch along that edge. Peel the tape off and then reuse it for the next line.

Joining wadding

Wadding is usually available in 90-100cm (35-39in) widths, so for large projects you will need to join pieces together. If you join wadding with a standard seam, you will get a bulky ridge in your quilt, so instead, the wadding should be butted together.

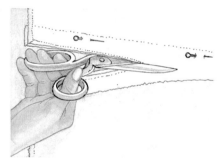

1 Cutting the wadding Overlap the two pieces of wadding by 2.5cm (1in) and pin the top edge with glass-headed pins – standard pins will get lost in the wadding. Using dressmakers' scissors, cut along the centre of the overlap, holding the scissors at a 45° angle for a mitred cut.

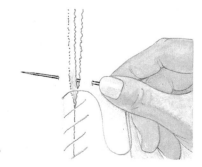

2 Stitching the wadding Butt the cut edges of the mitred pieces together. Using white thread, whipstitch the layers together.

Tacking the layers

On small projects you can tack the main fabric, wadding and backing together in one go, but on larger projects it is best to tack the wadding to the backing first, and then tack these to the top fabric.

1 Preparing the fabrics Fold the top fabric and backing fabric into quarters to find the centre points and mark them with pins. Press both fabrics to remove any creases.

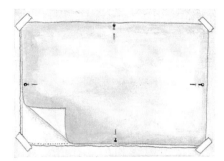

2 Positioning the backing Stick the corners of the wadding to the work surface or floor with masking tape. Lay the backing fabric on top, matching the centres and outer edges, and secure them with masking tape.

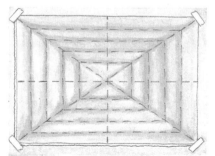

3 Tacking the backing Tack the two layers together, working diagonally outwards from the centre to each corner. Then tack from the centre outwards to the middle of each side edge. Now tack round the fabric in squares, again working from the centre outwards, and spacing the squares 7.5-15cm (3-6in) apart.

4 Tacking the top Remove the tape and turn the fabric layers over so that the wadding is on top. Tape the fabric layers centrally to the work surface. Put the top fabric centrally over the wadding. Tack the top fabric to the wadded backing, as in step 3. Avoid tacking over the quilting design lines.

Quilting a bedcover

When quilting an extra large project, such as a bedcover for a double bed, it is easiest to quilt it in sections.

To avoid centre seams, use a complete width of fabric for the top of the bed and half widths at either side. Seams should always run down the length of the quilt and should be symmetrical to produce a well-balanced appearance.

Place the machine on a large table or work top to give space for the fabric. Don't let the fabric hang over the side of the table as the weight will prevent you feeding the fabric evenly under the machine foot.

1 Cutting out the fabric Cut out the top of the cover and two side pieces, adding 1.5cm (⅝in) seam allowances for joining. Cut out the backing and wadding pieces to the same size, adding extra to the outer edges if the backing will be used to neaten the edges; join pieces if necessary (see JOINING WADDING). Pin and tack the three layers of each section together (see TACKING THE LAYERS).

2 Preparing the machine Set the machine for a medium-length stitch and loosen the tension. Fill the bobbin so it won't run out halfway through a line of stitching. If your machine has an adjustable speed, set it for the slowest speed. Test the stitch on a scrap of fabric and wadding.

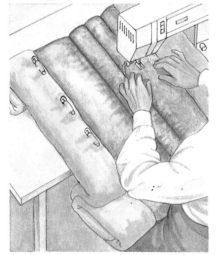

3 Starting to quilt Roll up two opposite sides of the fabric to make it easier to handle, and secure the rolls with safety pins. Sit at the sewing machine and fold each unrolled end into accordion pleats, with the front part folded on your lap. Start quilting at the centre, unfolding the fabric as necessary.

4 Finishing the quilting Unroll the next section of the quilt and then fold the ends as in step 3. Stitch this section. Continue in this way to quilt all of the first section, leaving the outer 5cm (2in) unstitched, and leaving long thread ends on the edges. Quilt the remaining pieces in the same way.

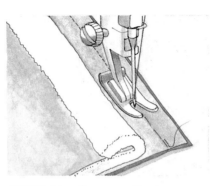

5 Stitching the cover Pin the top layers of the quilted sections together with the right sides facing and stitch only the top fabric pieces together, taking 1.5cm (⅝in) seam allowances.

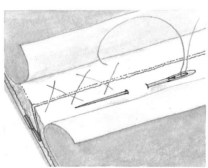

6 Neatening the back Trim the seam allowances on the top fabric and press the seams open. Trim off the excess wadding, mitring it so that the edges butt together along the seamline. Herringbone stitch or whipstitch the butted edges together. Tuck under the seam allowance on the backing fabric and slipstitch the two folded edges together over the join.

7 Completing the quilt Hand stitch any quilting lines that go across the seamlines using the ends of thread left hanging from the machine quilting. Finish the outer edges of the quilt with wide bias binding, or fold the backing fabric over to the right side to enclose all the raw edges and hem it.

Sink stitching

When you are quilting around patchwork shapes, you can hide the quilting stitches in the channel of the seams. This is called sink stitching. The stitches are only visible on the wrong side.

1 Preparing the layers Tack the fabric layers together. Pin into the channels of the seams in the top fabric to ease the fabrics apart and expose the seams. Put the pins in so that the heads of the pins will face you when you stitch to make them easy to remove.

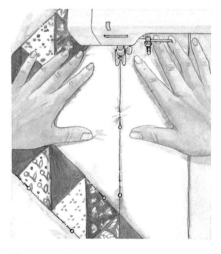

2 Working the stitches Start at one end of the fabric and stitch along the patchwork seams, holding the work flat and easing the seams open at the same time. When you release the fabric, the stitches will disappear into the channel. Work all the stitches in the same direction.

BOLD LINES
To emphasize your quilting pattern, thread two reels of matching cotton through the machine needle and stitch with both threads at once.

Log Cabin patchwork

*With clever strip-piecing methods, you can make a
Log Cabin quilt in just one day. Piece it together in one of
the many traditional geometric patterns.*

Log Cabin is one of the oldest patchwork designs, dating back to pioneering days in America. It is one of the most popular forms of patchwork, not least because it can be stitched quickly on a machine. The pattern is shown on page 116 as part of the sampler quilt. As a first project, try the development of the strip-piecing method, which enables you to make a Log Cabin quilt in just one day.

Once stitched in this speedy manner, the blocks can be pieced together in a variety of different ways to create dramatic patterns. Many patterns date from early colonial days when most homes had at least one Log Cabin quilt, and they have names that have been handed down for generations. The Fields and Furrows pattern, for example, represents the texture of a newly ploughed field, while Barn Raising (shown above) recalls the days when the women stitched quilts while the men

▲ *This soft blue and yellow Log Cabin quilt gives the appearance of being lovingly hand-crafted, but it can be made in a day.*

built barns. Turn to page 86 for these and other intriguing designs.

Instructions are for a quilt measuring 240 x 180cm (96 x 72in) – suitable for a single bed or as a throw for a double bed. You can adapt the size of the quilt by varying the width of the outer borders or adding extra rows of blocks.

Making a Log Cabin quilt in a day

To make the Log Cabin blocks, you need a total of seven different fabrics. Choose two basic colours which contrast well with each other, to emphasize the design created by the block arrangement. One will be your light colour and the other the dark. Choose fabrics with three graduating shades of each colour, then select a seventh fabric for the centres.

The finished blocks measure 30cm (12in) square and are pieced together without sashing strips. The fabric quantities are for a quilt using 24 blocks, and finished with three borders of different widths in the same way as the sampler quilt. Fabric quantities for the quilt top are for 112cm (44in) wide fabric. For the backing, choose a cotton fabric to tone with the quilt's colour scheme.

As for all machine patchwork, accuracy in cutting and stitching is essential for successful results. Use a rotary cutter, quilter's ruler and cutting mat to cut the fabric strips, and set up the machine to stitch accurate 7.5mm (¼in) seams.

Cutting out

Use a rotary cutter and quilter's ruler to cut exact strips. Fold the fabric with selvedges matching so that it fits on the cutting mat and cut all strips across the full width of the fabric.

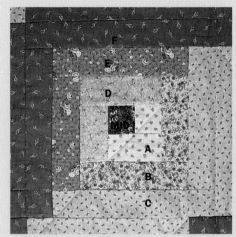

Following the diagram:
◆ Label the three light fabrics **A**, **B** and **C** and the three dark fabrics **D**, **E** and **F**.
From each of these fabrics, cut the following number of 6cm (2¼in) wide strips: **A** – 5 strips; **B** – 8 strips; **C** – 11 strips; **D** – 6 strips; **E** – 9 strips and **F** – 14 strips.

◆ From the seventh fabric chosen for the centre squares, cut two 6cm (2¼in) strips.

◆ For the borders:
For first border: cut 7 strips 9cm (3½in) wide.
For second border: cut 7 strips 11.5cm (4½in) wide.
For third border: cut 8 strips 14cm (5½in) wide.
For binding: cut 8 strips 3cm (1¼in) wide.

You will need

◆ **Seven fabrics for blocks:**
   25cm (10in) fabric for centres
   50cm (⅝yd) of fabric A
   50cm (⅝yd) of fabric B
   70cm (¾yd) of fabric C
   50cm (⅝yd) of fabric D
   70cm (¾yd) of fabric E
   1m (1⅛yd) of fabric F

◆ **70cm (¾yd) fabric for first border**

◆ **1m (1⅛yd) fabric for second border**

◆ **125cm (1⅜yd) fabric for third border**

◆ **40cm (15¾in) fabric for binding**

◆ **5m (5½yd) polyester wadding, 100cm (39½in) wide**

◆ **2.5m (2¾yd) cotton backing fabric, 180cm (72in) wide**

◆ **Rotary cutter, cutting mat and quilter's ruler**

◆ **Toning thread for stitching blocks**

◆ **Invisible nylon thread (optional)**

1 Laying out the fabrics Fold and arrange the block strips on the work table in the following order: centre, **A**, **D**, **B**, **E**, **C**, **F**. Each fabric, except the centre, is used twice in each block on adjacent sides.

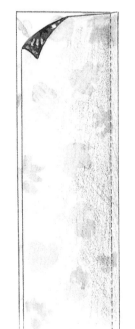

2 Stitching the centre blocks With right sides together, place a centre fabric strip on a strip **A**, with strip **A** underneath. Stitch a 7.5mm (¼in) seam down the right-hand edge. Repeat with second centre strip and another strip **A**. Do not open out.

6cm 2¼in

6cm 2¼in

6cm 2¼in

3 Cutting the centre blocks With the rotary cutter, cut the seamed strips into 24 6cm (2¼in) squares. Stack in a pile with wrong side of fabric **A** on top.

4 Joining second strip of A Lay a strip of **A** right side up on the machine. Open out a centre block and place right side down on **A** strip, and stitch right-hand edges together, finger pressing seam allowances upwards.

5 Completing second A strips Open out a second centre block. Butt it up to the first and continue stitching, finger pressing the seams upwards. Continue adding centre blocks until the strip runs out. Start a new strip of **A** and continue in the same way until all 24 centre blocks have been added. Lay strip on the cutting mat, block side up. Cut carefully between the blocks with a rotary cutter and stack the blocks so the strip just added is on top. Discard excess pieces of strip **A**.

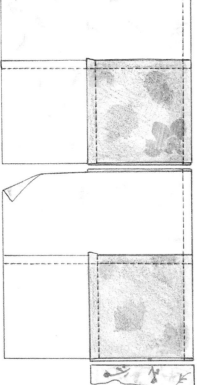

6 Joining first strip of D Lay a strip of **D** right side up on the machine. Open out a block and place it right side down on **D** strip. Rotate the centre square so that the last strip added is at the top and at right angles to the new strip. Stitch right-hand edges, finger pressing seam allowances upwards.

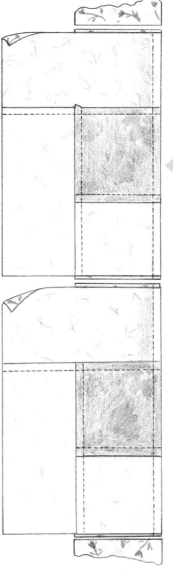

7 Finishing first strip of D As in step **5**, butt on the next block and continue until all blocks are stitched, starting new strips of **D** as necessary. Cut apart and stack with strip **D** on the top.

8 Adding second strip of D Lay a strip **D** and opened out block right sides together on the machine, rotating centre square so that last strip added is at top and at right angles to new strip. Stitch right-hand seam, finger pressing the first seam up and the second seam down. Butt up blocks and continue as in step **7** until all the blocks have been stitched. Cut apart and stack as in step **5**.

9 Stitching the next round Following steps **6-8**, add strips **B** then **E**, each time rotating the centre square and pressing the first seam up and the second down. Cut apart after each strip has been added, as in step **5**.

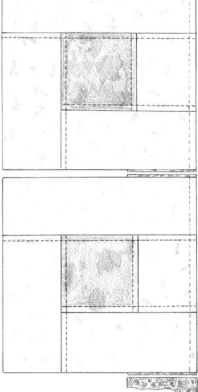

10 Completing the blocks Following steps **6-8**, add remaining strips **C** and **F**, stitching each fabric to two adjacent sides of the block and cutting apart after each strip has been added, as in step **5**. Press the finished blocks.

Making up the quilt

1 Choosing a pattern See below for design variations for making up the quilt, all using 24 blocks. Lay your blocks out on the floor, with four across and six down, following your chosen design.

2 Joining the blocks Stitch the blocks together in rows of four, pressing and laying each row back in place on the floor. Then stitch the rows together, making sure they are in the right order.

3 Stitching the borders Referring to page 125, steps **7-9**, attach the three borders. Press the quilt top.

4 Finishing the quilt Referring to page 126, step **4**, prepare the quilt for machine quilting. Using invisible nylon thread or a toning sewing thread, machine quilt the principle lines of the geometric pattern to highlight the light and dark areas. Then add the binding, as in steps **6-9**, using the 3cm (1¼in) wide strips already cut.

Pattern diagrams

Barn Raising

Zig-Zag

Arrow

Field and Furrows

Light Dominant

Dark Dominant

Patchwork sampler quilt

*Worked in easy stages, this machine stitched sampler
quilt quickly takes shape and will become an exquisite
heirloom for future generations to treasure.*

The technique of patchwork was originally devised for recycling old clothes and fabric remnants, turning them into warm quilts and other household items. This developed into an important craft form, with many traditional designs emerging.

Many of the popular designs we see today originated in America, where the early settlers formed groups to work on their patchwork together. Each person stitched a particular patchwork square, or block, often using designs brought from their home countries. The blocks were then sewn together into a quilt.

Traditionally stitched by hand, this type of block patchwork can also be worked very successfully on a sewing machine, with much quicker results. Many of the designs are based on simple, straight-edged, geometric shapes, such as squares and triangles, which are easy to machine stitch together. This is the method used to make the quilt shown here, which features twelve different patchwork block designs.

The following pages introduce you to the machine patchwork techniques, show how to stitch each block in turn, and suggest ways of using them in your home – as cushion covers, for example. Finally, you will learn how to join all

▲ *This single-bed quilt is made up of twelve blocks, each one showing a different traditional patchwork design.*

the blocks together, with machine quilting added to give extra surface interest and texture.

Instructions are given for two quilt sizes: a single-bed quilt, measuring 179 x 216.5cm (71½ x 86½in), made from 12 patchwork blocks; and a large double-bed quilt, measuring 216.5cm (86½in) square, made from 16 blocks. You can adapt the size of the quilt by altering the width of the outer borders.

Materials and equipment

Fabrics Patchwork is best made from 100% cotton fabrics. You can buy special patchwork cottons in a wide variety of colours and prints which blend well together. These quilt well, are treated with a crease-resistant finish and are virtually drip dry.

If you want to use remnants, make sure they are of the same weight with similar care qualities. Before starting, wash all the fabrics to check them for colourfastness and shrinkage. If a fabric 'bleeds', continue washing until it stops; if it does not stop, do not use the fabric.

Backing fabric and wadding Use 2oz washable polyester wadding for the quilt. For backing, choose one of your patchwork fabrics or a toning fabric of the same weight. Avoid sheeting and polyester fabrics, which can be tricky to quilt, and very dark fabrics, as the white wadding may show through.

Rotary cutter/mat and quilter's ruler These are essential items for cutting out patchwork pieces accurately.

Sewing machine No special sewing machine attachments are needed to work the patchwork. Check the upper and lower tensions on fabric scraps before you begin, to make sure the fabric doesn't pucker. Choose a stitch length of approximately 1.5mm (dial setting 2½) for sewing lightweight cotton, and use a needle size 80/12.

Thread Cotton thread is best for cotton fabric. Choose a colour that blends with the range of fabrics being used. You don't need to change threads when stitching different fabrics.

Fabric amounts

Fabric amounts are based on 112cm (44in) wide fabric, unless otherwise stated.

For a single quilt
◆ 50cm (⅝yd) of background fabric
◆ 30cm (⅜yd) of each of the other seven fabrics
◆ 1m (1⅛yd) fabric for sashing
◆ 90cm (1yd) fabric for first border
◆ 1.1m (1¼yd) fabric for second border
◆ 1.3m (1½yd) fabric for third border
◆ 4.5m (5yd) of 2oz polyester wadding, 100cm (39½in) wide
◆ 3.7m (4¼yd) backing fabric

For a large double quilt
◆ 1.2m (1⅜yd) of background fabric
◆ 70cm (¾yd) of each of the other seven fabrics
◆ 2m (2½yd) fabric for sashing
◆ 90cm (1yd) fabric for first border
◆ 1.1m (1¼yd) fabric for second border
◆ 1.3m (1½yd) fabric for third border
◆ 6.7m (7¾yd) of 2oz polyester wadding, 100cm (39½in) wide
◆ 4.5m (5yd) backing fabric

Terms used in patchwork
Block Completed square section of patchwork design.
Sashing Pieces of fabric used between the blocks to join them together.
Border Bands of fabric added to the outer edges of the completed piece of patchwork to frame it.

Choosing fabrics

With such a vast array of fabrics available, the task of choosing colours and patterns that work well together can seem daunting. A few basic principles will help to make it easier.

First, think about the setting in which the quilt is to be used. You might wish to create a soft and pretty look, or one that is rich and dramatic. Decide on a general colour range.

When you're ready to get down to specifics, start by choosing the quilt's background fabric. Remember that there will be a lot of this, so use a soft colour, either plain or with a pattern that is not too strong.

Next choose a range of fabrics that blend and tone with one another, adding interest and depth with different sized prints as well as plains. Choose prints with all-over designs that are not too widely spaced, and include one fabric with a stronger tone than the rest. As a beginner, avoid checks, stripes and one-way designs as these can be difficult to work with. Don't limit yourself to too few fabrics – the quilt shown here uses seven in addition to the background fabric.

Preparing the machine

Accurate measuring, cutting and stitching is essential for the success of any block patchwork project. The quilt featured here has a 0.75cm (¼in) seam allowance throughout. Follow these steps to make sure that your machine stitches this accurately every time, using a piece of masking tape as a seam guide. Alternatively, use a shop-bought seam guide.

Note that, for ease of use, the metric and imperial measurement equivalents given here are rounded up, rather than precise; it is therefore essential to keep to one or the other throughout the sewing project – mixing the two will mean that the blocks won't piece together accurately.

1 Marking on the seam allowance On a piece of paper, mark a line exactly 0.75cm (¼in) from one straight edge. Place the paper under the machine foot, and insert the needle on the pencil line.

2 Applying the tape Stick a piece of masking tape to the machine, butting it right up against the right-hand edge of the paper, so that when you stitch along the pencil line, the paper runs smoothly alongside the tape.

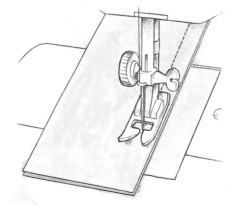

3 Stitching a sample Cut three pieces of fabric, 12.5 x 4cm (5 x 1½in). With right sides together and edges matching, stitch two pieces together down one long side, running the edge of the fabric alongside the masking tape. Repeat to add the third piece of fabric, then press with the seam allowances lying one way.

▲ *Cast casually over a sofa or armchair, a patchwork quilt in tones of pink, green and cream adds a splash of colour and a comfortable, homey air to a sitting room.*

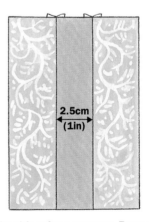

2.5cm (1in)

4 Checking for accuracy From the right side, measure across the central fabric piece from seam to seam. It should measure exactly 2.5cm (1in). If it measures less, the seam allowance is too large; if it measures more, the allowance is too small. Adjust the tape if required, and try again until the measurement is correct. Use the tape as a seam guide throughout the patchwork project.

Patchwork sample blocks

Below are the twelve blocks that make up the main body of the quilt. Each is shown with the sashing around it, though this is not added until the making-up stage.

Ohio Star (A)

Prairie Queen (B)

Roman Pin Wheel (C)

Rocky Mountain Puzzle (D)

Card Trick (E)

Album (F)

Milky Way (G)

Bow Ties (H)

Dutchman's Puzzle (I)

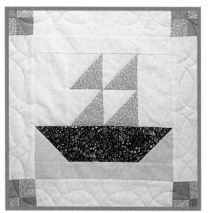

Sail Boat (J)

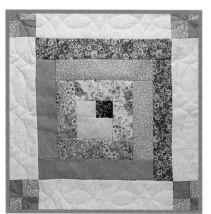

Log Cabin (K)

Land of the Midnight Sun (L)

Patchwork quilt – block A

The popular Ohio Star design forms the first block of the patchwork sampler quilt. Use pretty fabric scraps to stitch a practice block, which you can then make into an attractive cushion cover.

Ohio Star is a truly traditional American block patchwork design, made up from square and triangular patches, usually in four different fabrics. It's known as a nine-patch block because the final block is made up from nine main segments, each one consisting either of a single patch or of a few patches stitched together. The segments are joined in rows of three, which are in turn stitched together to make up the finished block. Several of the other designs featured in the sampler quilt are nine-patch blocks.

If you're new to machine patchwork, it's a good idea to practise the technique by making up each block for the quilt in some spare fabrics before you embark on the real thing. You can either use leftover scraps of fabric or buy a coordinating range especially – remember the patchwork samples need never be wasted. Here, for example, they're made into cushion covers, adding a homey touch to a sofa, chair or bed.

Each finished block measures 30cm

▲ *Practise your machine patchwork technique by stitching a sample Ohio star block from fabric remnants, then make it into a cushion cover.*

(12in) square. To make one into a 42cm (17in) square cushion cover, simply add a double border round the edge using the same or toning fabrics. This also frames the design in much the same way as the sashing on the quilt.

Stitching the Ohio star block

To form the Ohio star design, you need a total of *four* fabrics, including the background fabric. When selecting the fabrics, bear in mind that the objective is for the star design to stand out from the background.

If you want to make the Ohio star block into a cushion cover, follow the steps overleaf to add borders, using the same fabrics as you used for the patchwork, or different, toning fabrics. Instructions are also given on how to machine quilt the design for added surface texture. If you're making the block as the first square of your patchwork quilt, do not quilt it at this stage.

When stitching together the patches, take an exact 7.5mm (¼in) seam allowance. Don't fasten off thread ends – just trim them, leaving about 2cm (¾in) free. Take extra care when stitching bias seams, guiding the fabric through gently so as not to distort it.

After every step in the construction of the block, place the pieces back in position on the table. This will help to avoid mistakes in assembling them.

You will need

To make a cushion cover:
- ◆ Four different cotton fabrics
- ◆ 45cm (18in) square of 4oz washable polyester wadding
- ◆ 45cm (18in) square of cotton backing fabric
- ◆ 60 x 43.5cm (24 x 17½in) piece of fabric for the cushion back
- ◆ 40cm (16in) square cushion pad
- ◆ Rotary cutter and cutting mat
- ◆ Ruler and quilter's square
- ◆ Pins and toning thread

Cutting out: Ohio star

Use a rotary cutter to cut out the pieces. The quarter-square triangles are cut from a 13.5cm (5¼in) square to allow for the additional seam allowances needed. When you have cut all the pieces, place them on a table in the correct position and check that you are happy with the arrangement of colours and prints. The pieces will not seem to fit at this stage because of all the additional seam allowances.

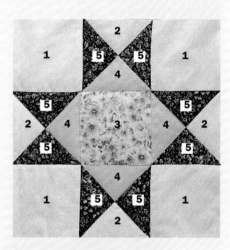

Following the diagram above:
For **1:** Cut four 11.5cm (4½in) squares from background fabric.
For **2:** Cut one 13.5cm (5¼in) square from background fabric, and cut across on both diagonals giving four triangles.
For **3:** Cut one 11.5cm (4½in) square.
For **4:** Cut one 13.5cm (5¼in) square, and cut across on both diagonals giving four triangles.
For **5:** Cut two 13.5cm (5¼in) squares. Cut each across on both diagonals, giving eight triangles.

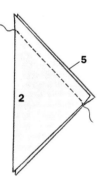

1 **Stitching the small triangles** Right sides together, place a triangle 2 on top of a triangle 5. Stitch diagonal seam as shown. Repeat with the other three pairs of 2 and 5.

2 **Pressing the seams** Repeat step **1** to assemble triangles 4 and 5. On each pair of triangles, press the seam allowances in opposite directions, preferably to the darker of the two fabrics, after stitching.

PRESSING

Tip

Always press patchwork with a firm, downward pressure. Don't iron backwards and forwards as this can stretch bias seams and distort the final shape of the block. Press the seam allowances together, towards the darker of the fabrics where possible.

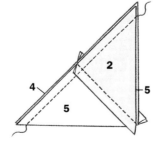

3 **Forming a square** Right sides together, pin together the 2-5 and 4-5 triangles, pinning at right angles to stitchline. Check centre seams match on right side, and seam allowances lie in opposite directions. Stitch.

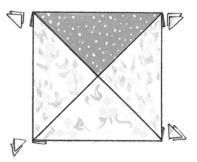

4 **Trimming the seams** Open out the squares and press the seam allowances to one side. Trim protruding seam allowances level with the corners. Lay squares in position.

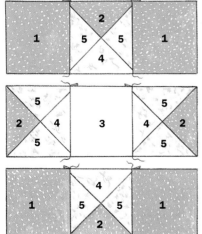

5 Stitching the squares together
Pin, then stitch the squares together in three rows of three squares each. Press the seam allowances to one side and place the rows back on the table in the correct positions.

6 Stitching the rows together Pin, then stitch the rows of squares together in the right order, making sure that the seams line up with each other exactly. Press the seam allowances to one side.

▲ *Experiment with your chosen fabrics to see how they can work together to create different effects.*

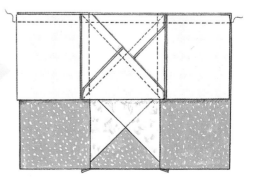

Making up the cushion cover

These steps show how to make the Ohio Star patchwork block into a cushion cover. As all the patchwork blocks for the quilt measure 30cm (12in) square, you can use these instructions to make future practice blocks into cushions in the same way – for yourself or as gifts for friends.

The borders framing the patchwork are 1cm (½in) wide and 5cm (2in) wide. You can adapt them if you wish to make a slightly larger or smaller cushion. The measurements in the cutting out instructions (see step **1**) include a 7.5mm (¼in) seam allowance.

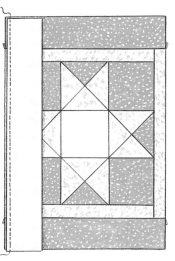

1 Cutting out the border strips
For the inner border: cut two strips 31.5 x 2.5cm (12½ x 1in), and two strips 33.5 x 2.5cm (13½ x 1in).
For the outer border: cut two strips 33.5 x 6.5cm (13½ x 2½in), and two strips 44.5 x 6.5cm (17¼ x 2½in).

2 Stitching the inner border Take the shorter, narrow strips. With right sides together, pin to opposite edges of the patchwork block, matching the edges exactly. Machine stitch and press turnings towards the border. Attach the longer narrow strips to the other two edges of the block in the same way. Press.

3 Stitching the outer border Repeat the process with the wide strips. Pin the shorter strips to two opposite edges of the inner border. Machine stitch and press turnings towards the outer border. Pin and stitch the longer strips in place in the same way. Press again. The cushion cover front should now measure 43.5cm (17½in) square.

4 Machine quilting (optional) Cut a piece of 4oz washable polyester wadding and one of lightweight cotton backing fabric slightly larger than the cushion front. Sandwich the wadding between the cushion front and the backing fabric, right sides out, and pin and tack in position. Using invisible thread, machine quilt along the seamlines of the patchwork pieces.

5 Finishing the cushion front Replace the invisible thread with ordinary thread and work a line of small zigzag stitch all round the edges of the cushion front. Trim away excess wadding and backing fabric.

▼ *Lightly machine quilting the panel seams of the cushion cover emphasizes the patchwork design and gives a professional looking finish.*

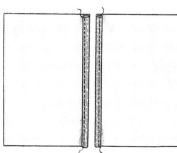

6 Preparing back Cut two panels of fabric 43.5 x 30cm (17½ x 12in). Turn in and machine stitch a narrow double hem down one long side of each piece. Press the hems.

7 Stitching back With right sides together pin the two back pieces to the cushion cover front, matching the outer edges to the front edges and overlapping the two hemmed edges. Machine stitch. Clip the corners and turn right sides out. Press lightly.

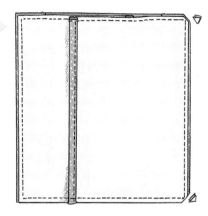

Patchwork quilt – block B

*Use furnishing fabrics in muted shades of rose and
cream to make the Prairie Queen block into an elegant
table runner with a traditional Victorian feel.*

The Prairie Queen block is the next block in the sampler quilt. It is a nine-patch block. The pieces are assembled into nine squares, and these squares are joined to make the finished block. It combines the strip-piecing and grid-piecing techniques, two methods that make quick work of an apparently complicated block. Use the block for your sampler quilt, or alternatively you could stitch them together and add borders and a backing to make a runner with a charming old-fashioned feel.

Furnishing fabrics can work well in machine-stitched patchwork, but they do need some special handling. For example, although a rotary cutter will cope well with cutting them out, you'll find thicker fabrics more difficult to use in blocks which include very small pieces in their construction.

▲ *A patchwork runner protects your table from marks, as well as adding an air of elegance reminiscent of Victorian days.*

Before starting to stitch, insert a stronger needle in your machine and consult the operating manual on how to stitch thicker fabrics. To avoid bulk-iness, make sure the seam allowances lie in opposite directions when making up the block, and press firmly at each stage.

Stitching the Prairie Queen block

The Prairie Queen block uses a total of four fabrics, including the background fabric. For the patchwork quilt, shown on pages 87–90, the central square of the block is cut from the background fabric. For the runner, shown on the opposite page, it is cut from the same fabric as the large inner triangles. The cutting measurements include a 7.5mm (¼in) seam allowance, and the machine needs to be set up to stitch this distance accurately.

Cutting out: Prairie Queen block

Use a rotary cutter and cutting mat, and a quilter's ruler, pencil and set square to cut the squares, rectangles and strips. When cutting the long strips, fold the fabric in half with the selvedges together so that it will fit on the cutting board.

For **1**: Cut one 11.5cm (4½in) square from the background fabric.
For **2**: Cut a piece of background fabric 28 x 15cm (11 x 6in).
For **3**: Cut a piece 28 x 15cm (11 x 6in) from one of the three remaining fabrics.
For **4** and **5**: Cut a strip 56 x 6.5cm (22 x 2½in) from each of the remaining two fabrics.

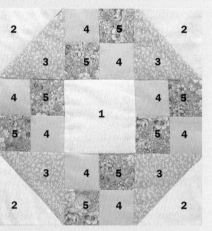

You will need

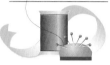

- ◆ Four different 145cm (57in) wide furnishing fabrics: – 50cm (⅝yd) for backing and inner border; 40cm (½yd) for outer border and central square; 20cm (¼yd) of remaining two fabrics
- ◆ Matching thread
- ◆ Rotary cutter and cutting mat
- ◆ Quilter's ruler and set square

1 Grid-piecing the corner squares With a pencil, ruler and a set square, draw a grid of two accurate 12.5cm (4⅞in) squares on the wrong side of the large piece of background fabric. See page 104, *Stitching the Milky Way block*, steps **1-3**, for marking out the grid, stitching the triangles and cutting out. You will have four triangle-squares composed of triangles **2** and **3**.

2 Stitching the strips With right sides together, stitch the strips for **4** and **5** with a 7.5mm (¼in) seam allowance. Press the seam allowance to the darker fabric, laying the strip across, not along, the ironing board and pressing with short movements to avoid distorting the pieced strip.

3 Cutting the pieced strip Using the rotary cutter and quilter's ruler, straighten one end of the pieced strip. Cut across the strip in 6.5cm (2½in) sections to give eight identical pieces. Line up the horizontal line of the ruler with the centre seamline before cutting each piece.

4 Stitching the pieced squares Stitch the cut sections together in pairs to give four four-patch squares. The seam allowances will automatically be going in opposite directions to provide accurate matching of seams at the centre of the pieced square.

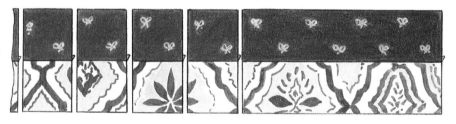

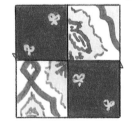

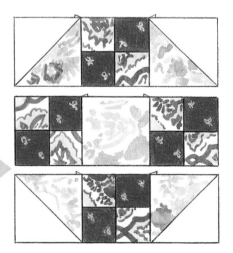

5 Assembling the block Lay out all the pieces, including the centre square, in their correct positions. Then stitch them together in three rows, as with other nine-patch blocks. Press the seam allowances of each row in opposite directions.

▶ *Here, rich red and old gold tones have been selected to complement the polished surface of a dining table or sideboard. Using furnishing-weight fabric adds substance to the runner.*

6 Completing the block Stitch the three rows together, making sure that all the seams line up with each other accurately. Press the finished block carefully.

Making the table runner

This unique and attractive patchwork runner would make a perfect centre-piece for your dining table, or for a dressing table or chest of drawers in the bedroom. Either way, choose four furnishing fabrics to coordinate with the decor of your room. If you use your block to make cushion covers, tie up your choice of fabrics to link with those; matching curtain tiebacks could carry out your colour scheme further.

Remember to take an exact seam allowance of 7.5mm (¼in) when making up the runner. The finished runner measures 100 x 40cm (40 x 16in).

1 Making two matching blocks
Follow the instructions on the previous page to make two identical Prairie Queen blocks.

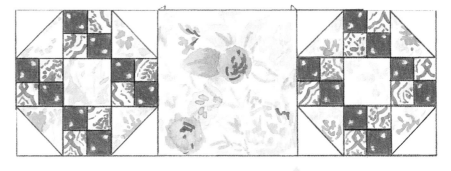

2 Cutting out *For the centre square:* cut one 31.5cm (12½in) square. *For the inner border:* cut two strips 91.5 x 2.5cm (36½ x 1in), and two strips 33.5 x 2.5cm (13½ x 1in). *For the outer border:* cut two strips 93.5 x 5.5cm (37½ x 2in), and two strips 41.5 x 5.5cm (16½ x 2in). *For the backing:* cut a rectangle 101.5 x 41.5cm (40½ x 16½in).

3 Joining the pieces
Place the two blocks on the table on either side of the centre square. Stitch them together and press the seam allowances towards the centre square.

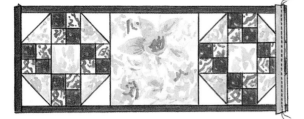

▼ The double border unifies the three blocks and creates a strong, defining outline. You could make the runner shorter by adding additional squares at each end. Alternatively, use this idea plus additional blocks to make a tablecloth, or throw for a bed.

4 Stitching the inner border With right sides together, pin and stitch the long narrow strips to the long edges of the runner. Press the seam allowances towards the border. Attach the short narrow strips to the short edges of the runner in the same way. Press.

5 Adding the outer border Repeat step **4** to add the wide border strips, attaching the long strips to the long sides first and pressing the seam allowances outwards.

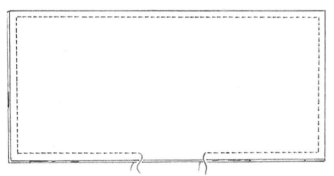

6 Stitching the backing Place the backing and runner right sides together. Machine stitch all round, leaving a 20cm (8in) opening in one long edge. Trim the corner seam allowances: turn out, pushing out the corners gently with a pencil point. Press. Slipstitch the opening closed.

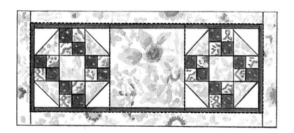

7 Finishing the runner With the right side of the runner facing, machine stitch in the ditch all round the inner edge of the wide border, and again on the seamlines between the squares.

Tip

FABRIC RANGES
Take the stress out of selecting fabrics for the runner by using a selection from a coordinating range, as shown here.

Patchwork quilt – blocks C and I

*Two more blocks from the patchwork quilt join
forces in a colourful table cloth which will bring a touch
of bright Mediterranean sunshine to your table.*

The next two blocks in the sampler quilt are the Roman Pin Wheel (C) and the Dutchman's Puzzle (I). Both are four-patch blocks: this means that the units are pieced together into four squares, and these squares are then joined to form the finished block.

While you are making up the blocks,

you will learn two more techniques used in machine-stitched patchwork. The strip-piecing method is used to create the striped effect in the Roman Pin Wheel block, and the Dutchman's Puzzle uses so-called Flying Geese units.

The cutting measurements for both blocks include the usual 7.5mm (¼in)

seam allowance. It is important that your sewing machine stitches this amount accurately, so follow page 89 to check that it is correctly set up. To avoid making mistakes when you are assembling the blocks, lay the pieces back in position on the table between each step in the construction.

*Choose bold colours,
like these vivid blues and
yellows, to make two each
of your next two sampler
blocks, and stitch them into
a cheerful table cloth.*

Making the Roman Pin Wheel

The Roman Pin Wheel block uses an important patchwork technique – the strip-piecing method. Long strips of fabric are stitched together and then cut into triangles. These are then joined to form the design. The Roman Pin Wheel block uses five fabrics, including the background fabric.

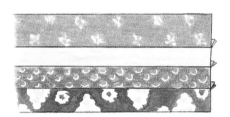

1 Stitching the strips Lay out the strips in your chosen sequence, with the 5cm (2in) wide strip at the top. Stitch with right sides together, sewing the seams in alternate directions to prevent the pieced strip bowing. Press all the seam allowances in the same direction.

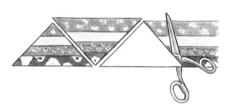

2 Cutting the strip-pieced triangles Place the paper template on the strip-pieced fabric, with the point of the triangle on the outer edge of the wider strip. Cut round the template carefully. Repeat three more times to give four identical strip-pieced triangles.

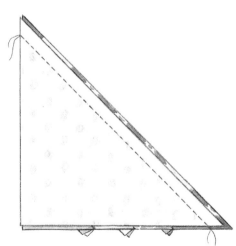

3 Forming the squares With right sides together and matching raw edges, stitch a plain triangle to a strip-pieced triangle to give a square. Repeat three more times to give a total of four squares. Snip across corners and press seam allowances towards the strip-pieced triangle.

Cutting out: Roman Pin Wheel

Use a rotary cutter, quilter's ruler and cutting mat for cutting out. To cut long strips, fold the fabric in half, with selvedges matching, so that it fits on the cutting mat.

Following the diagram, right:
For **1**: From the background fabric, cut two 17.5cm (6⅞in) squares. Cut across each square once diagonally to give four triangles. Draw round one triangle to make a paper template.
For **2**: From each of three fabrics, cut a strip 115 x 4cm (45 x 1½in).
For **3**: From remaining fabric, cut a strip 115 x 5cm (45 x 2in).

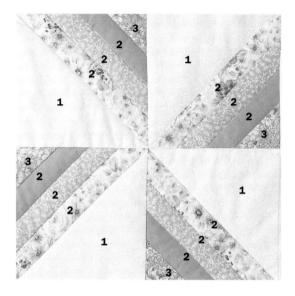

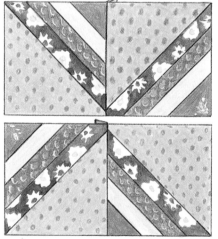

4 Joining the squares Lay the squares out in their correct positions. With right sides together, pin, then stitch the squares together in two pairs. Then pin and stitch the pairs together to form the finished block, making sure that the seams line up exactly.

5 Pressing the finished block Unpick two stitches above the final seam so that the seam allowances will lie flat at the centre of the finished block. Press.

Tip

PRESSING STRIPS
The seams on a pieced strip can distort when they are pressed. To avoid this, lay the strips across, not along, the ironing board and press with short movements.

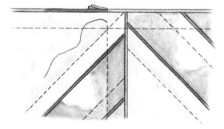

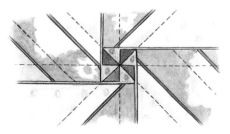

Making the Dutchman's Puzzle

Like several other patchwork blocks, the Dutchman's Puzzle includes Flying Geese units. These have a large triangle (the goose) and two smaller triangles (the sky). When they are joined, they form a rectangle. For the Dutchman's Puzzle design, you'll need five fabrics including the background fabric.

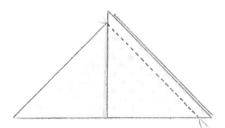

1 Stitching the Flying Geese units Right sides together, stitch the long side of a small triangle **1** to the short side of a large triangle **2**, matching the corners at the base of the large triangle. Repeat, using the continuous stitching method for the remaining units. Snip the units apart and press the seam allowances towards the small triangle.

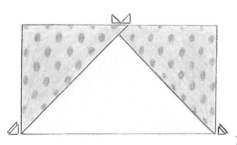

2 Completing the units Right sides together, stitch the long side of a small triangle **1** to the other short side of large triangle **2**, matching the corners at the base of the large triangle. Repeat, using the continuous stitching method for the remaining units. Press seam allowances towards small triangles and trim away points.

Cutting out: Dutchman's Puzzle

Use a rotary cutter, quilter's ruler and cutting mat to cut out the squares and triangles. Place the cut pieces in their correct position on the table to check that the design works in your fabrics.

Following the diagram right:
For **1**: From the background fabric, cut eight 10cm (3⅞in) squares. Cut across each square diagonally to give sixteen triangles.
For **2**: From each of the four remaining fabrics, cut one 13cm (5⅛in) square. Cut across each square diagonally, to give eight triangles.

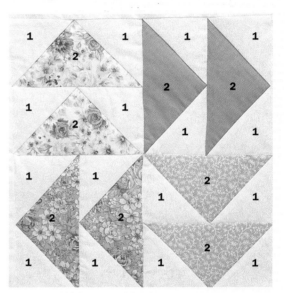

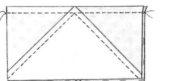

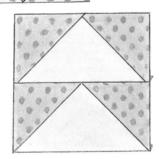

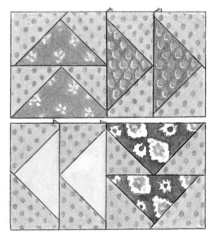

Tip

BIAS EDGES
Triangles with bias edges need handling gently. When stitching them, don't pull the fabric but let the machine do the work. You should also take care not to stretch the seams when pressing. Press seams with a downward pressure – do not iron from side to side.

3 Forming the squares Place two matching units right sides together, matching the top of one unit to the bottom of the other (so that the large triangles point in the same direction when opened out). Stitch together, with the point of the large triangle on top to make sure that the stitching goes through the point. Repeat with the remaining three pairs of Flying Geese to make four squares. Press the seam allowances towards the base of the large triangle.

4 Joining the squares Stitch the squares together in pairs, making sure that the large triangles lie in the right direction. Stitch the pairs together to complete the block, making sure that the seams line up exactly, with the seam allowances pressed in opposite directions. Give the completed block a final press.

Making the table cloth

The Dutchman's Puzzle and the Roman Pin Wheel blocks work well together in a cheerful patchwork table cloth. Make up your cloth in a sunny mix of boldly coloured Provençal cottons – you will need five fabrics, including a background fabric. Remember to take an exact 7.5mm (¼in) seam allowance throughout. The finished table cloth measures 125cm (50in) square.

You will need

◆ **70cm (³⁄₄yd) of background fabric**

◆ **50cm (⁵⁄₈yd) each of four cotton prints, 156cm (60in) wide**

◆ **Rotary cutter, cutting mat and quilter's ruler**

1 Making the blocks Following the instructions on the previous two pages, make two Roman Pin Wheel blocks and two Dutchman's Puzzle blocks. Use the same background fabric for all four blocks.

3 Joining the pieces Lay all the cut pieces and blocks on the floor with the large square in the centre. Place matching blocks in opposite corners and matching rectangles on opposite sides. Join the pieces together in three rows. Press seam allowances in opposite directions. Lay the rows back in place on the floor.

2 Cutting out *For the table cloth:* cut a 46.5cm (18½in) square from the background fabric, and two rectangles 46.5 x 31.5cm (18½ x 12½in) from each of two other fabrics. *For the inner border:* cut four strips 115 x 4cm (45 x 1½in). *For the outer border:* cut four strips 130 x 9cm (50 x 3¾in).

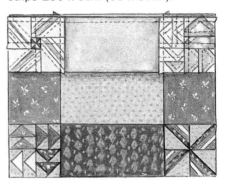

4 Joining the rows Pin, and then stitch the rows together in the right order, making sure that the seams line up with each other exactly. Press seam allowances to one side.

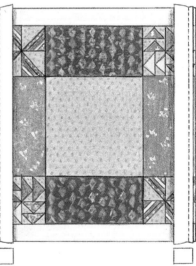

5 Stitching the inner border Right sides together, pin a narrow strip to two opposite edges of the table cloth. Machine stitch. Trim off excess strip and press the seam allowances towards the border. Repeat to attach the remaining narrow strips to the other two edges of the cloth. Press.

6 Stitching the outer border Repeat step **5** to stitch on the wide border strips. Press. To finish, press, and then machine stitch a 7.5mm (¼in) double hem all round the outer border. Give the table cloth a final press.

◀ *Bright Provençal cottons evoke memories of warm climates and summer meals outdoors.*

Sampler quilt – blocks D and G

*The magical grid-piecing technique makes quick work of
the next two blocks of the patchwork sampler quilt – you'll be
delighted at the speed and accuracy of the results.*

The Rocky Mountain Puzzle (D) and the Milky Way (G) introduce you to a new method of working machine stitched patchwork, called grid-piecing. This method – used for joining two triangles to form a square – involves stitching the fabrics before cutting them out, rather than the other way round. It's the best way of piecing small triangles, which are hard to handle individually.

A grid is drawn on the wrong side of one fabric, which is pinned to a second fabric. The marked lines are stitched and the pieces are cut apart to reveal a shape known as a triangle-square.

▼ *Although it looks more complicated, the Rocky Mountain block (bottom) is just as easy as the Milky Way block (top) – the secret being accurate piecing together.*

Preparing to stitch

In addition to a rotary cutter, cutting mat and quilter's ruler, you will need a pencil and set square. As before, all the cutting measurements for both blocks include a 7.5mm (¼in) seam allowance. Before you start to construct the blocks, make sure that your sewing machine will stitch this amount accurately by following page 89. Wherever possible, remember to press seam allowances to the darker fabric.

Stitching Milky Way block

The Milky Way design uses a combination of a background fabric and a second fabric for the star. The star fabric should be one that stands out well against the background.

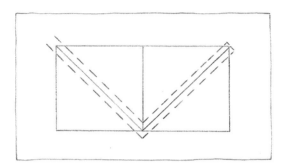

1 Marking out the grid Using the pencil, ruler and set square, draw a grid of two accurate 12.5cm (4⅞in) squares on to the wrong side of the large piece of background fabric. Draw a diagonal line across each square. These are all cutting lines. Draw a dotted line to mark the stitching lines 7.5mm (¼in) each side of the diagonal cutting lines.

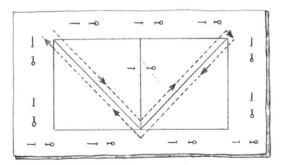

2 Stitching the triangles With the right sides together, place the marked out fabric on the star fabric. Pin them securely together, placing the pins away from the stitching lines. Make sure that the two layers lie together smoothly, with the straight grains matching. Machine stitch along the stitching lines in the direction of the arrows.

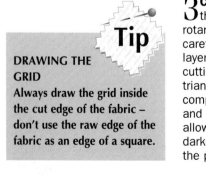

Tip

DRAWING THE GRID

Always draw the grid inside the cut edge of the fabric – don't use the raw edge of the fabric as an edge of a square.

3 Cutting out Remove the pins. Then, using a rotary cutter and ruler, cut carefully through both layers of fabric along the cutting lines, giving four triangle-squares composed of triangles 3 and 4. Press the seam allowances towards the darker fabric and trim off the protruding corners.

Cutting out: Milky Way

Use a rotary cutter to cut out accurate squares. The triangles are marked on to the wrong side of the fabric and then cut out after stitching.
Following the diagram below:
For **1**: Cut four 11.5cm (4½in) squares from the background fabric.
For **2**: Cut one 11.5cm (4½in) square from the star fabric.
For **3** and **4**: cut one piece approximately 28 x 15cm (11 x 6in) from both the background and star fabrics.

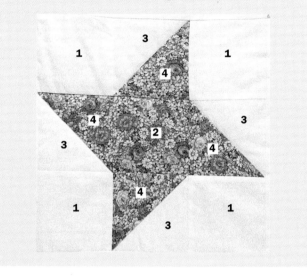

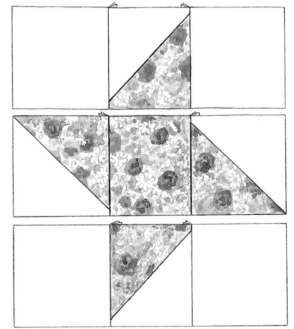

4 Assembling the block Lay out all the squares and triangle-squares in their correct positions, using the cutting out picture as a guide for placement. Stitch them together in three rows, checking that the points of the star lie in the right direction. Press the seam allowances of each row in opposite directions.

5 Completing the block Stitch the three rows together, making sure that all the adjoining seams line up with each other accurately. Press the finished patchwork block.

Stitching the Rocky Mountain Puzzle block

Cutting out: Rocky Mountain

Use a rotary cutter to cut out the squares and rectangles accurately. The triangles are marked out on the fabric and stitched before cutting out.

Following the diagram below:
For **1**: Cut one 11.5cm (4½in) square from the first contrast fabric.
For **2**: Cut two rectangles 11.5 x 4cm (4½ x 1½in) from second contrast fabric.
For **3**: Cut two rectangles 16.5 x 4cm (6½ x 1½in) from second contrast fabric.
For **4**: Cut two 9cm (3½in) squares from background fabric.
For **5**: Cut a piece 33 x 23cm (13 x 9in) from background fabric.
For **6**: Cut a piece 33 x 23cm (13 x 9in) from the third contrast fabric.

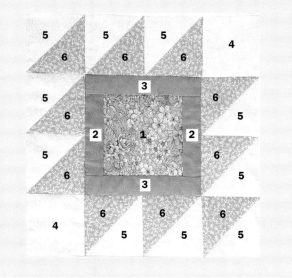

The Rocky Mountain Puzzle design uses three contrasting fabrics in addition to the background fabric. When constructing the block, lay all the pieces out in their correct places, pick up the pieces as you need to stitch them and then replace them, to avoid making mistakes in assembling them.

1 Stitching the centre square
With right sides together, stitch a rectangle 2 to opposite edges of square 1. Press the seam allowances to the darker fabric, then stitch the rectangles 3 to the remaining edges of the square. Press seams.

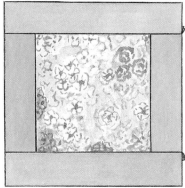

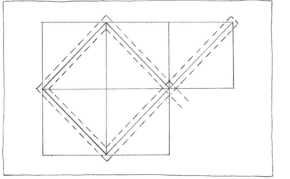

2 Marking out the grid On the wrong side of the large piece of background fabric, use a pencil, ruler and set square to draw a grid of five accurate 10cm (3⅞in) squares – three across and two down. Draw a diagonal line across each square. These are all cutting lines. Draw a dotted line to mark the stitching lines 7.5mm (¼in) each side of the diagonal cutting lines.

Tip

MATCHING THE SEAMS
To match the adjoining seams accurately, reduce the thickness by pressing one set of seam allowances in one direction and the other set in the opposite direction.

◄ *The Rocky Mountain block falls on the left-hand side of the quilt, next to the Ohio Star, Milky Way and Card Trick blocks.*

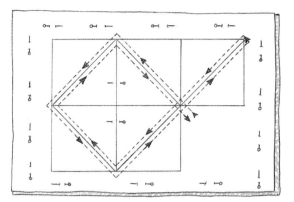

3 Stitching the triangles With right sides together, place the marked out fabric on the piece of fabric chosen for triangles 6. Pin together, placing the pins away from the stitching lines. Make sure that the two layers lie smoothly with the straight grains matching. Machine stitch along the stitching lines in the direction of the arrows.

4 Cutting the triangle-squares Remove the pins. Using a rotary cutter and ruler, cut through both layers of fabric along all the cutting lines, giving ten triangle-squares composed of triangles 5 and 6. Press seam allowances towards the darker fabric. Trim off the protruding corners.

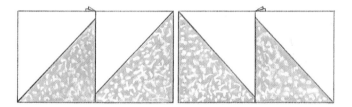

5 Stitching the triangle-squares together Stitch eight triangle-squares together to make four pairs. The triangles 6 lie in one direction for two of the pairs, and in the opposite direction for the remaining two pairs. This leaves two triangle-squares unused at this stage.

▲ *The distinctive, pointy shapes of a triangle-square are an integral part of the Rocky Mountain and Milky Way blocks. They are both made using the grid-piecing method and rely on accurate piecing of the triangle-squares at the final making up stages.*

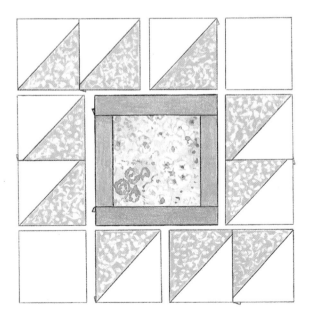

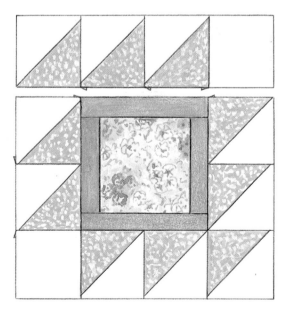

6 Assembling the block Place all the pieces, including the centre square, in their correct positions on the table. Stitch the pieces that make up the top and bottom rows together, using the spare triangle-squares and the two squares 4. Place back in position on the table.

7 Completing the block Stitch the remaining pairs of triangle-squares to opposite sides of the central square, checking that all the triangles 6 lie in the right direction. Add the top and bottom rows to complete the block, matching all the seams accurately.

Patchwork quilt – block E

The intriguing Card Trick design forms the next block of the patchwork sampler quilt. Made up in the same fabrics, your practice piece is an attractive companion to the Ohio Star cushion cover.

The interlocking components of the Card Trick design produce an intriguing three-dimensional effect to the block. Like the Ohio Star – the first block of the quilt – it is a nine-patch block which uses triangular shapes in its construction. In the case of the Card Trick, half-square triangles are used as well as quarter-square triangles.

Similar in construction, these two block designs complement one another beautifully, so why not make your Card Trick patchwork practice piece from the same fabrics you used for the Star. Then use it to create a matching cushion cover – placed side by side on a sofa, easy chair or bed, they'll add a touch of country-style comfort to a room.

The Card Trick uses four different fabrics *in addition to* the background

▲ *Show off your practice blocks for the Ohio Star and Card Trick designs by making them up into cushion covers. The two designs are constructed in a similar way, so they sit well together.*

fabric. To bring out the three-dimensional effect, choose four fabrics which contrast strongly with one another and stand out well against the background.

Making the Card Trick block

When stitching the patches together, use an exact 7.5mm (¼in) seam allowance and take care not to distort the fabric on bias seams. Always place the pieces back in their correct positions on the table after every step in the construction of the block, to avoid making mistakes when stitching them together.

To find out what materials you need and instructions on how to make your practice piece into a cushion cover, see pages 92-94.

1 Stitching the corner squares Right sides together, place a triangle 1 on top of a triangle 4. Stitch the diagonal seam. Repeat with the other pairs of 1 and 4. Press and place back in position on the table.

2 Stitching the centre square Take one triangle 3 of each of the four fabrics, and stitch together to form a square, as for the Ohio Star block on page 92, steps **1-4**. Place back in position on the table.

3 Starting remaining four squares Right sides together, place a triangle 2 on top of a triangle 3. Stitch one straight seam. Repeat with the other three pairs of 2 and 3. Press and place back in position on table.

Cutting out: Card Trick

Use a rotary cutter to cut out the pieces, following the instructions and measurements right. Place the cut pieces in their correct positions on the table to check that the arrangement of fabrics gives a good three-dimensional effect.

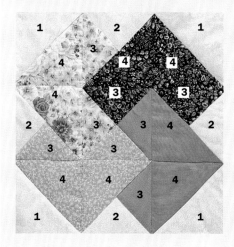

Following the diagram left:
For **1**: From the background fabric, cut two 12.5cm (4⅞in) squares. Cut across each square once diagonally to give four triangles.
For **2**: From the background fabric, cut one 13.5cm (5¼in) square. Cut across on both diagonals to give four small triangles.
For **3**: From each of the four remaining fabrics, cut one 9.5cm (3¾in) square. Cut across each square once diagonally to give two small triangles in each fabric.
For **4**: From each of the same four fabrics, cut one 12.5cm (4⅞in) square. Cut across each square once diagonally to give two large triangles in each of the four fabrics.

4 Completing a square Right sides together, place one triangle 2/3 on top of a triangle 4, and stitch the diagonal seam, making sure all corners and edges line up accurately.

5 Stitching the squares together Check that all the squares are in their correct places. Pin, then stitch together in three rows of three squares each, making sure all corners meet exactly. Place rows back on table. Pin, then stitch rows together, checking that the seams line up accurately.

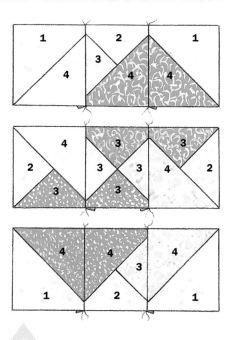

◄ *These two cushions show how easy it is to achieve a variety of three-dimensional effects using different combinations of the same fabrics.*

Sampler quilt – blocks F and H

*The next two blocks of the patchwork sampler
quilt – the Album and Bow Ties – make perfect table mats,
worked in a mixture of smart black and white prints.*

The next two blocks of the sampler quilt are the Album (F) and the Bow Ties (H). The Album block was originally designed as a so-called 'friendship' block – people would sign their names in the rectangular shapes which are the main feature of the design. It is constructed in a different way to the other blocks in the quilt. Instead of square units being pieced together, a large pieced triangle is stitched to each side of a central strip to make the final square block.

The Bow Ties block is wonderfully quick to construct using the continuous stitching method. Four individual bow tie motifs are stitched together to make a single block for the quilt, but you could make a wonderful scrap quilt or throw, entirely from Bow Ties, as each motif takes only small pieces of fabric.

As always, it is important to ensure

▲ *In chic black and white, these two table mats have a smart contemporary feel – despite the fact that they are based on two very traditional patchwork block designs, the Album and Bow Ties.*

that your machine will stitch accurately the 7.5mm (¼in) seam allowance included in the cutting measurements for both blocks. Follow page 89 to set up your machine to do this.

Stitching the Album block

Cutting out: Album

Use a rotary cutter, quilter's ruler and cutting mat to cut out accurate squares, triangles and rectangles. If your ruler does not have $\frac{1}{16}$in markings, $\frac{5}{16}$in is between $\frac{1}{4}$in and $\frac{3}{8}$in, and $\frac{3}{16}$in is between $\frac{1}{8}$in and $\frac{1}{4}$in.

Following the diagram, right:
For **1**: From the main contrasting fabric, cut four rectangles 15.5 x 8.5cm ($6\frac{3}{16}$ x $3\frac{5}{16}$in).
For **2**: From the main contrasting fabric, cut two 7.5cm ($2\frac{7}{8}$in) squares, and cut across each once diagonally giving four triangles.
For **3**: From the second contrasting fabric, cut four 8.5cm ($3\frac{5}{16}$in) squares.
For **4**: From the background fabric, cut two 13.5cm ($5\frac{1}{4}$in) squares, and cut across each on both diagonals to give eight triangles.
For **5**: From the background fabric, cut one 8.5cm ($3\frac{5}{16}$in) square.

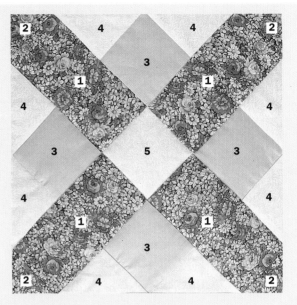

The Album block uses only two fabrics in addition to the background fabric. Between each step, always place the pieces back in position on the table to ensure they are in the correct positions.

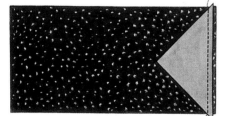

1 Stitching the rectangles Finger press a crease at centre of each rectangle. Right sides together, and lining up points of triangle on crease, stitch a triangle 2 to one end of each rectangle. Press seams towards triangles and trim off corners.

2 Piecing large triangles Stitch a triangle 4 to two sides of each square 3, matching right angle of triangle to corner of square (tips of triangle will extend beyond edges of square). Press seam allowances towards triangle and trim off corners.

3 Finishing large triangles Stitch a triangle made in step **2** to each side of a rectangle unit made in step **1**, matching the corners of the triangles to the corners of the rectangles. Press the seam allowances towards the triangles, and trim off the protruding corners.

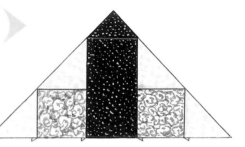

4 Stitching the centre strip Stitch the remaining two units made in step **1** to opposite sides of the background square 5. Press the seam allowances towards the square.

5 Finishing block Stitch a large pieced triangle to each side of the centre strip, making sure that the seams line up accurately. Press the seam allowances towards the triangles.

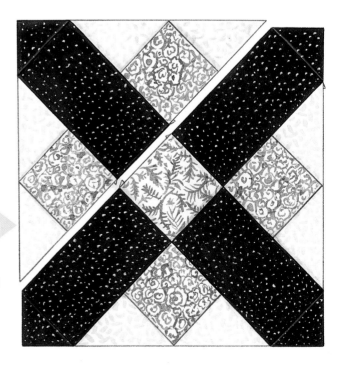

Stitching the Bow Ties block

To make the finished 30cm (12in) square block for the sampler quilt, four bow tie motifs are stitched and then joined together. You will therefore need four different fabrics in addition to the background fabric. The block is quickly constructed using the continuous stitching method.

Cutting out: Bow Ties

Use a rotary cutter, quilter's ruler and cutting mat to cut accurate squares and triangles.

Following the diagram, right:
For **1**: From the background fabric, cut eight 9cm (3½in) squares.
For **2**: From each of four different fabrics, cut two 9cm (3½in) squares.
For **3**: From each of the same four fabrics, cut two 5.2cm (2in) squares.

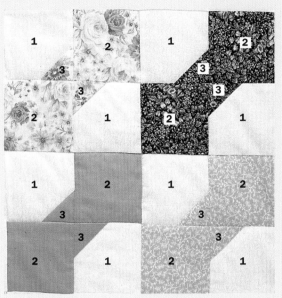

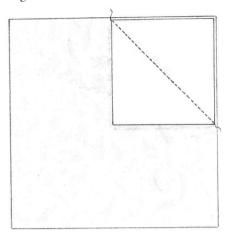

1 Stitching the centres of the bows
Fold the small 5.2cm (2in) squares in half diagonally and gently finger press to leave a crease. Place a small square 3 on top of a background square 1, right sides together with corners matching. Stitch along the creased line. Repeat, using the continuous stitching method, so that each background square 1 has a small square 3 sewn to it.

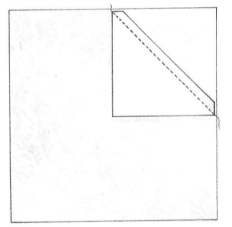

2 Finishing the centres of the bows
Trim the small squares back to leave a 7.5mm (¼in) seam allowance. *Do not* trim the corners of the background squares – these are needed to ensure that the final block is square. Press the corner triangles over the background squares.

3 Stitching the bow ties Lay out two pieced squares and two matching bow tie squares 2. Stitch the squares together in two pairs, then stitch the pairs together, with the seam allowances lying in opposite directions where they meet at the centre. If the small triangles are not lined up exactly with the background squares, use the background fabric as a guide for stitching the 7.5mm (¼in) seam allowance. Repeat to make the three remaining bow ties.

4 Finishing block
Lay out the four bow ties, making sure that they are all lying in the same direction. Stitch them together in pairs, and then stitch the pairs together to complete the block. Make sure that the seams line up exactly, with seam allowances at centre of the block lying in opposite directions. Press the finished block.

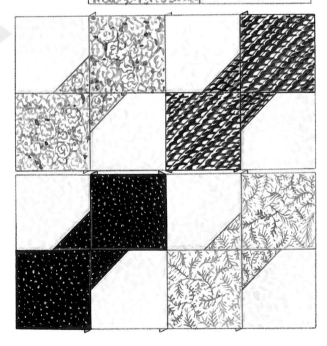

Making the table mats

For either design you will need four different fabrics, one of which will be used for the backing and edge binding. The mats are machine quilted to give extra insulation and protect the table surface. Ordinary polyester wadding would be too puffy for the mats, so use polyester needlepunch wadding for a firmer finish. The finished table mats measure 49.5 x 31.5cm (19½ x 12½in).

1 Making a block Following the cutting and making up instructions on the previous two pages, make up either the album patchwork block or the bow ties patchwork block.

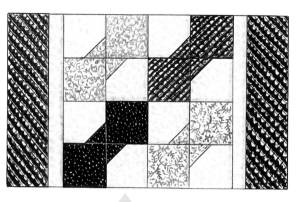

You will need

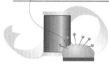

For each mat:

◆ **Four different printed cotton fabrics – 20cm (¼yd) of three, and 40cm (½yd) of the fourth**

◆ **Needlepunch polyester wadding 54 x 34cm (21 x 14in)**

◆ **Nylon invisible thread**

2 Cutting out *For narrow side strips:* from background fabric, cut two strips 31.5 x 4cm (12½ x 1½in). *For wide side strips:* from contrasting fabric, cut two strips 31.5 x 8cm (12½ x 3in). *For binding strips:* from backing fabric, cut two strips 49.5 x 3.5cm (19½ x 1¼in), and two strips 31.5 x 3.5cm (12½ x 1¼in). *For the backing:* from backing fabric, cut a piece 49.5 x 31.5cm (19½ x 12½in).

3 Stitching the side strips With right sides together, stitch a narrow side strip to opposite edges of the block, taking a 7.5mm (¼in) seam allowance. Press the seam allowances towards the strips. Add the wide side strips in the same way, stitching one to each narrow strip.

4 Machine quilting the mat Cut a piece of needlepunch wadding to same size as the finished patchwork mat. Tack the wadding between the mat and the backing, as described on page 79, steps **1-2**. Using invisible nylon thread, machine quilt around the patchwork pieces, and on the seamline between the narrow and wide side strips. Trim edges to neaten.

◀ *Choose the smallest mini prints, and subtle self-colour designs to make the most of the witty Bow Ties and Album blocks.*

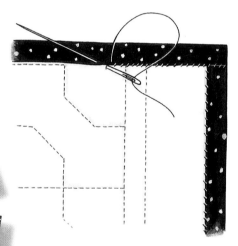

5 Binding the edges On each edge strip, press a 7.5mm (¼in) turning to the wrong side on both long edges. Apply these straight binding strips in the same way as bias binding, matching the edges of the mat and binding strip. Stitch the long strips first and then the short strips. Neaten the ends of the short strips.

Patchwork quilt – block J

In addition to being a charming part of the patchwork sampler quilt, the Sail Boat block works well as a picture in its own right. Made into a wall hanging in bright primary colours, it will become a favourite item in a child's room.

As a separate panel, the Sail Boat block from the patchwork quilt makes an ideal wall hanging to brighten up a small child's bedroom. It looks especially cheerful if you choose fabrics in the bold primary colours that children love. You just need to add borders and hanging loops, and machine quilt the outline of the boat to give the finished picture extra definition.

The design for the Sail Boat uses four different fabrics. Make sure that the fabrics you select for the hull and sails stand out well against the sea and sky fabrics. The block is simply constructed from two different sized rectangles plus half-square triangles. Before stitching, place all the pieces in their appropriate positions on a flat surface to check that the fabrics work well together.

▲ *With matching borders and loops added, the Sail Boat patchwork panel makes an easy-to-hang framed picture. A witty choice of starry fabric for the sky, sunny yellow sails and a scarlet, white-dotted hull bobbing on a royal blue sea, conjures up a jolly sailing scene.*

Making the Sail Boat block

The cutting measurements include a 7.5mm (¼in) seam allowance throughout. Prepare your machine for accurate stitching, following page 89. Press the seam allowances towards the darker fabric where possible.

1 Stitching the sails With right sides together, place each sky triangle 3 on top of a sail triangle 4. Stitch the diagonal seams, giving four squares. Press and trim off protruding corners.

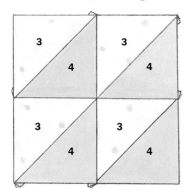

2 Joining the sails Stitch sail/sky squares together in rows of two squares, check sails face in same direction. Stitch rows together. Press.

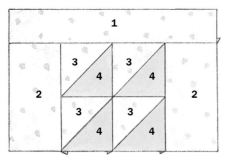

3 Attaching the sky Stitch a rectangle 2 to each side of the sails. Press. Stitch the long, thin rectangle 1 to the top edge. Press.

4 Stitching the hull With right sides together, place each hull triangle 6 on top of a sea triangle 7. Stitch diagonal seams, giving two squares. Press. Stitch the hull side of a hull/sea square to each end of hull rectangle 5. Press.

5 Completing the block Stitch the long, thin sea rectangle 8 to the bottom of the boat, making sure that the boat is the right way up. Stitch the boat section to the sails/sky, matching the vertical seams. Press.

Cutting out: Sail Boat

Cut out following the diagram below:
For **1**: From the sky fabric, cut one rectangle 31.5 x 5.25cm (12½ x 2in).
For **2**: From the sky fabric, cut two rectangles 16.5 x 9cm (6½ x 3½in).

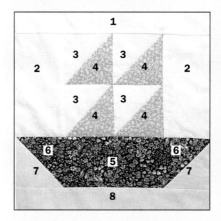

For **3**: From the sky fabric, cut two 10cm (3⅞in) squares. Cut across each square once diagonally, giving four triangles.
For **4**: From the sail fabric, cut two 10cm (3⅞in) squares. Cut across each square once diagonally, giving four triangles.
For **5**: From the hull fabric, cut one rectangle 16.5 x 9cm (6½ x 3½in).
For **6**: From the hull fabric, cut one 10cm (3⅞in) square. Cut across the square once diagonally, giving two triangles.
For **7**: From the sea fabric, cut one 10cm (3⅞in) square. Cut across the square once diagonally, giving two triangles.
For **8**: From the sea fabric, cut one rectangle 31.5 x 5.25cm (12½ x 2in).

You will need

To make a wall hanging:

- ◆ Four different cotton fabrics
- ◆ 51cm (20in) square of 60g (2oz) washable polyester wadding
- ◆ 60cm (24in) cotton fabric for backing, outer border and hanging loops
- ◆ 10cm (4in) of cotton fabric for inner border
- ◆ Rotary cutter and a cutting mat
- ◆ Quilter's ruler

Making up the wall hanging

1 Adding borders Cut out and attach borders, following page 94, steps **1-3**.

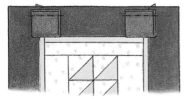

2 Making hanging loops Cut two pieces 15 x 7.5cm (6 x 3in) from outer border fabric. Right sides together, stitch down each long side. Cut in half widthways, turn right sides out and press. Fold each strip in half and, with raw edges matching, tack to right side of panel top edge, 5cm (2in) in from each side.

3 Finishing the hanging Cut backing fabric to the same size as the panel. Lay out wadding and place Sail Boat panel and backing fabric, right sides together, on top. Taking a 7.5mm (¼in) seam allowance, pin and stitch all round, leaving an 18cm (7in) gap in the bottom edge. Trim away excess wadding, turn right side out and slipstitch the opening closed. Machine quilt the outline of the boat and sails.

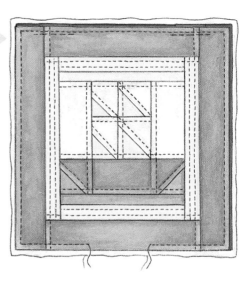

Patchwork quilt – block K

*The Log Cabin design is one of the best known and simplest
forms of patchwork. Strips of fabric are stitched into squares which
make striking geometric patterns when pieced together.*

Log Cabin was a popular form of patchwork during the second half of the nineteenth century, both in England and America. It is simple and quick to do and retains its popularity today. It is traditionally made up of an equal number of light and dark fabrics graduating out from a central square. The division between light and dark runs diagonally across the block, and the design relies for its effect on the shading this creates. The central square symbolises fire, with the

light half of the block representing the side of the room lit by the fire, while the dark half of the design represents the side of the room in shadow.

The straight strips used to build up the Log Cabin design are all cut to the same width and are trimmed to the right size as you work. The Log Cabin design is one of the blocks used in the sampler quilt, but it can also be pieced together in a variety of intriguing geometric patterns to create eye-catching quilts or throws.

▲ *A collection of well-loved soft toys finds an attractive setting on a Log Cabin quilt. The blocks are all made the same and then pieced together in a striking geometric pattern.*

Stitching the Log Cabin block

To make the Log Cabin block, you need a total of seven different fabrics. Select three light fabrics and three dark fabrics, to graduate out from a central square cut from the seventh fabric. When stitching the strips together, take an accurate 7.5mm (¼in) seam allowance to ensure that all the strips are exactly at right angles to each other and that the finished block is square. These instructions are for a finished block measuring 30cm (12in) square.

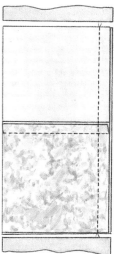

1 Joining first strip With right sides together, place the centre square on to strip **A**, matching the right-hand edges. Stitch. Trim the strip, leaving two squares joined together. Open out and then press the seam allowances towards **A**.

2 Joining second strip of A Right sides together, place stitched block on remaining strip of **A**, with **A** at the top and matching right-hand edges. Stitch. Trim the strip above and below the stitched block. Press seam allowance towards **A**.

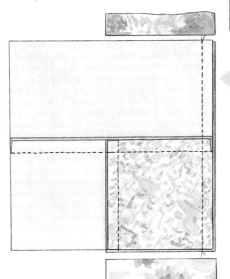

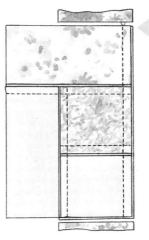

3 Joining first strip of D With right sides together, place the stitched block on **D**, with the long section of **A** at the top and at right angles to **D**. Matching the right-hand raw edges, stitch along seam. Trim the strip above and below the stitched block and then press the seam allowance towards **D**.

4 Joining second strip With right sides together, place the stitched block on the remaining strip of **D**, with the long section of **D** at the top. Matching the right-hand edges, stitch the seam. Trim the strip above and below the stitched block. Press the seam allowance towards **D**.

5 Stitching next round Continue in the same way, following steps **3** and **4** above to join strips **B** and **E** to the stitched block. Join all the pieces right sides together, trim the strips and then press seam allowances towards the strip you have just stitched.

6 Completing the block For the third round of the Log Cabin design, follow steps **3** and **4** above to join the remaining light and dark strips of fabric – strips **C** and **F**. Remember that each fabric is stitched to the block on two adjoining sides. When the patchwork block is completed, press carefully.

Tip

STRAIGHT EDGES
Before cutting out the pieces for any patchwork block, it is important to straighten the cut edge of the fabric and make sure that it lies at right angles to the selvedge.

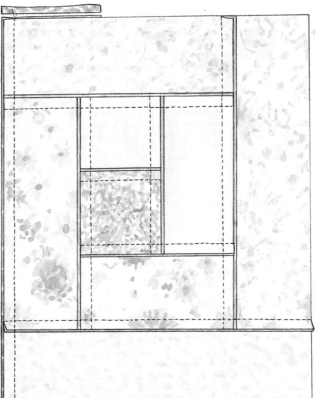

Cutting out: Log Cabin

Use a rotary cutter and quilter's ruler to cut strips of exactly the same width, following the instructions and measurements below.

Following the diagram, right:

◆ Label the three light fabrics **A**, **B** and **C** and the three dark fabrics **D**, **E** and **F**. From each of these six fabrics, cut a strip 6cm (2¼in) wide and as long as possible from the width of your fabric. If you are using remnants of fabric, the maximum length needed for a single strip is 34cm (13½in).

◆ From the seventh fabric, chosen for the centre square, cut one 6cm (2¼in) square.

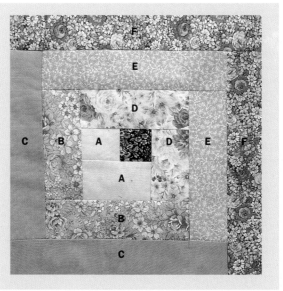

▼ *Use a selection of coordinating fabrics echoing a chosen colour theme to make a pretty Log Cabin throw. Stitch the blocks together randomly for a charming country cottage effect. Instructions for making the throw are given overleaf.*

Making a patchwork throw

You can piece the Log Cabin blocks together in a multitude of arrangements, using the light and dark shading to create striking geometric effects. For a more subtle effect, choose fabrics which do not contrast too strongly with each other. Coordinate the colours with existing soft furnishings by incorporating remnants of curtain fabric into the design.

The instructions here are for a finished throw measuring approximately 94 x 124cm (37⅓ x 49½in) – a good size for a sofa throw or a quilt for a child's bed. It's made up of twelve Log Cabin blocks, with a narrow 2cm (¾in) border. If you want to make a larger quilt, just add more squares and adapt the width of the border to fit.

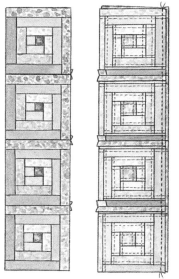

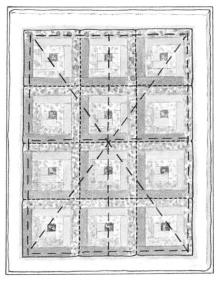

You will need

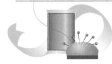

- ◆ **Cotton fabrics in different colours for the patchwork**

- ◆ **40cm (½yd) of 120cm (48in) wide patterned cotton fabric for the border**

- ◆ **98 x 128cm (38 x 50in) rectangle of lightweight calico, preshrunk, to back the quilting**

- ◆ **98 x 128cm (38 x 50in) rectangle of mediumweight wadding**

- ◆ **98 x 128cm (38 x 50in) rectangle of plain cotton fabric for backing**

- ◆ **Matching sewing thread**

- ◆ **Ruler**

1 Joining the squares Follow steps 1-6, *Stitching the Log Cabin block*, to make 12 blocks. Lay them out, right sides up, in a rectangle four squares deep and three squares wide. Right sides together and taking a 7.5mm (¼in) seam, stitch the squares together in three vertical strips of four squares. Press seams open. Right sides together, stitch down long edges to join strips. Press.

3 Adding the backing Centre the backing fabric, wrong side down, on top of the calico. Then, working outwards from the centre, tack through all the layers and around the outside edge. Trim backing fabric, calico and wadding 1.2cm (½in) away from edges of the patchwork.

4 Cutting out the border Measure the short ends of the cover and cut two 8cm (3in) wide strips to this length. Measure the long edges of the cover, add 3cm (1¼in) and cut two 8cm (3in) wide strips to this length, joining strips if necessary.

2 Adding the wadding Place the wadding on the lightweight calico and then centre the joined patchwork squares, right side up, over the wadding. Working from the centre outwards, pin then tack through all layers. Topstitch through all layers along the seamlines joining each patchwork square. Remove tacking stitches.

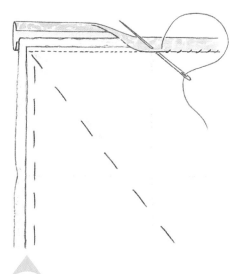

5 Attaching top and bottom borders Right sides together, pin and then stitch a short border strip 2cm (¾in) in from short edge of throw. Fold strip to back of cover, turn under 2cm (¾in) along raw edge and slipstitch to previous line of stitching. Repeat to stitch remaining short border strip.

6 Attaching side border strips Stitch the long strips to the sides of the cover in the same way, stitching over the ends of the short border strips. Turn in the ends of long strips at each corner and slipstitch in place. Remove all remaining tacking stitches. Press.

Patchwork quilt – block L

*The rich, warm colours of Indian carpets make a
glowing fashion accessory featuring the block known
evocatively as the Land of the Midnight Sun.*

Appearances can be deceptive – although the patchwork block, Land of the Midnight Sun, looks complicated, it is in fact another nine-patch block. At its centre it has a star shape similar to the Milky Way block (see pages 103-104). The construction of Land of the Midnight Sun uses some of the simple steps that you have already tried in other blocks. You will also learn how to use a cut-off template to modify a half-square triangle into a trapezoid shape.

The secret of success for this block lies in the careful choice and placement of fabrics which should bring out an eye-catching effect of interlocking squares.

When choosing furnishing fabrics for patchwork, it's best to avoid using very thick or loosely woven fabrics – the seam allowances will fray easily, making neat piecing difficult. Needlecord adds a rich texture and its weight works well with many furnishing fabrics.

▶ *Practise your patchwork
skills by making two
Land of the Midnight
Sun patchwork blocks –
it's easier to do than it
looks. Then you can
display your handiwork
and put it to good use by
making this large and
roomy shoulder bag.*

Stitching Land of the Midnight Sun block

The Land of the Midnight Sun block uses a total of *five* different fabrics, including the background fabric. To make the most of the effect of inter-locking squares, make sure that one of your fabrics makes a strong contrast with the other four.

All the cutting measurements given below include a 7.5mm (¼in) seam allowance. To set up your sewing machine to stitch this allowance accurately, refer to page 89.

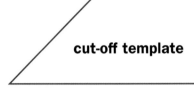

cut-off template

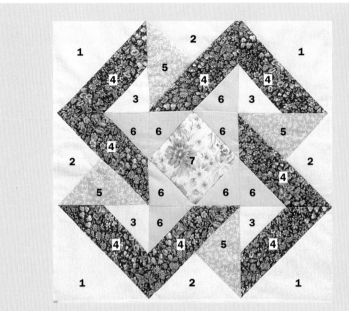

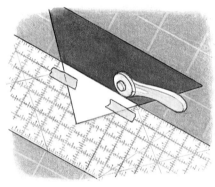

1 **Cutting the trapezoid shapes** Trace the cut-off template (above) on to stiff paper; cut it out. Tape template to the quilter's ruler, with long edge of triangle aligned to edge of ruler. Position template over point of each triangle 4 and trim off right-angled corner, giving eight trapezoid shapes.

Cutting out: Land of the Midnight Sun

Use a rotary cutter, cutting mat and quilter's ruler to cut the squares and triangles. You will also need tracing paper, a pencil, and a piece of stiff paper for making a cut-off template.

After cutting out the block pieces, lay them out on the table in their correct order to check the effective-ness of the colour placement. Always lay the pieces back in place between each stage of the construction process to avoid mistakes.

For **1**: Cut two 12.5cm (4⅞in) squares from background fabric. Cut each square once diagonally to give four triangles.
For **2**: Cut one 13.5cm (5¼in) square from background fabric. Cut across on both diagonals to give four triangles.
For **3**: Cut two 7.5cm (2⅞in) squares from background fabric. Cut across each square once diagonally to give four triangles.
For **4**: Cut four 12.5cm (4⅞in) squares from the dominant fabric. Cut across each square once diagonally to give eight triangles.
For **5**: Cut one 13.5cm (5¼in) square. Cut across on both diagonals to give four triangles.
For **6**: Cut four 7.5cm (2⅞in) squares. Cut across each square once diagonally to give eight triangles.
For **7**: Cut one 8.5cm (3⅜in) square.

2 **Starting the corner squares** With right sides together, position the diagonal edge of a background fabric triangle 3 to the shorter edge of a trapezoid. Stitch to form a large triangle. Press the seam allowances to the darker fabric.

3 **Completing the corner squares** With right sides together, position a large background fabric triangle 1 to a 4/3 triangle. Stitch the diagonal seam to form a square, then press the seam allowances to the darker fabric. Repeat three times.

4 **Starting the side squares** To the remaining four trapezoids, stitch a small triangle 6 to form a large triangle, as in step **2**. Right sides together, position a triangle 5 to a background fabric triangle 2 and stitch together along one short side. Repeat three times. Press.

▲ *With careful choice and placement of fabrics in the patchwork, the effect of the Land of the Midnight Sun block will be of interlocking squares.*

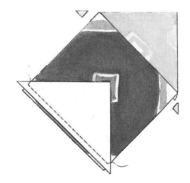

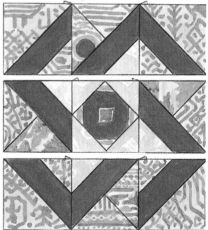

5 Completing the side squares With right sides together, position a 4/6 triangle to a 5/2 triangle. Stitch the long diagonal seam to form a square. Press. Repeat three times.

6 Stitching the centre square With right sides together, position the diagonal side of a small triangle 6 to opposite sides of square 7 and stitch. Trim off protruding corners and press seam allowances to the darker fabric. Stitch the remaining two triangles 6 to the other sides of the square. Press.

7 Assembling the block You now have nine pieced squares. Lay them out in their correct positions on the table. Stitch the squares together in three rows of three. Press seam allowances in opposite directions on each row. Stitch the rows together, checking that seams line up exactly.

Making the shoulder bag

The finished bag is 46cm (18½in) square – plenty big enough to carry your belongings with ease. The front and back panels are machine quilted to give the bag body, and the handles are just the right length to allow the bag to sit comfortably on your shoulder.

If you use needlecord, play with the pieces after cutting them out to check on the effect of placing the pile in different directions – the light will catch it and change the depth of the colour.

You will need

- ◆ **1.5m (1⅝yd) needlecord, 112cm (44in) wide, for the dominant patchwork pieces and main bag fabric**
- ◆ **30cm (⅜yd) of furnishing fabric, 148cm (58in) wide, for the background**
- ◆ **20cm (¼yd) each of two other furnishing fabrics, 148cm (58in) wide**
- ◆ **8.5cm (3⅜in) square piece of fabric for centre square**
- ◆ **Thread to tone with the main fabric**
- ◆ **Fine nylon invisible thread**
- ◆ **1m (1⅛yd) of 100g (4oz) washable polyester wadding**
- ◆ **Two pieces of cotton backing fabric, 50cm (19¾in) square**

1 Making the blocks Following the instructions on the previous two pages, make two identical Land of the Midnight Sun blocks.

2 Cutting out *For the inner borders:* cut four 40 x 2.5cm (16 x 1in) strips, each from two different fabrics. *For the outer border:* from main fabric, cut four 48 x 7.5cm (20 x 2¾in) strips. *For the bag lining:* from main fabric, cut two 47.5cm (18½in) squares. *For the handles:* cut two 61 x 11.5cm (24 x 4¼in) strips from main fabric. *From the wadding:* cut two 50cm (19¾in) squares.

3 Stitching the inner borders With right sides together, pin matching narrow border strips to opposite edges of patchwork block. Machine stitch, taking a 7.5mm (¼in) seam allowance. Trim off excess strip at ends and press seam towards border. Repeat to attach remaining matching strips to the other two edges of the block. Attach the four strips for second narrow border in the same way.

4 Stitching the outer border Repeat step **3** to stitch the outer border to the edge of the inner border. Press.

5 Machine quilting the panels Tack each wadding square between a front panel and a backing fabric square, as described on page 79, steps **1-2**. Using invisible nylon thread, machine quilt round the central star and interlocking strips, and round outer edge of patchwork block and inner edge of wide border.

6 Finishing the panels With ordinary thread, work a medium-sized zigzag stitch through all the layers, 1cm (⅜in) from outer edges of each panel. Trim away the excess wadding and backing fabric.

7 Stitching the bag With right sides together, pin, then stitch the two panels together, taking a 1cm (⅜in) seam allowance and leaving one edge open. Clip corners, press side seams open and turn right sides out. Press.

8 Stitching the handles Turn in and press 7.5mm (¼in) to the wrong side on long edges of handle strips. Match the folded edges together and topstitch close to both long edges of handles. Matching raw edges, tack handles to outside of the bag, placing them 9cm (3½in) from sides of bag.

9 Stitching the lining With right sides together, pin and stitch the lining squares together on three sides, taking a 1cm (⅜in) seam allowance and leaving a 20cm (8in) opening in the centre of the bottom edge. Clip corners and press side seams open.

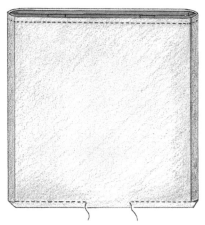

10 Finishing the bag With right sides together, insert the bag inside the lining. Pin the top edges together and stitch, taking a 1cm (⅜in) seam allowance. Turn the bag to right side through the opening in the lining and slipstitch the opening closed.

Finishing the sampler quilt

*With all twelve blocks completed, finally it is time
for the quilt to come together. Add sashing and borders
and your beautiful heirloom will be finished.*

*Your patchwork
quilt will bring
a delightful air
of old-world
charm to your
bedroom.*

Completing the patchwork sampler quilt

These instructions are for a single bed quilt made with twelve blocks. For a double bed quilt, you will need sixteen blocks, nine extra sashing strips and five more four-patch blocks. For details of suitable fabrics, see page 88.

You'll need a large area to lay out the blocks – the floor is ideal. Accuracy is essential, so use a rotary cutter, quilter's ruler and cutting mat to cut out; refer to page 89 to see how to machine stitch accurate 7.5mm (¼in) seams.

The sashing is made of plain fabric strips, intersected by four-patch squares at each corner of the blocks. These four-patch squares are made with the same strip-piecing method used for the Prairie Queen block, page 96.

There are three borders of graduating widths. You can adapt the finished size of the quilt by changing the width or number of the borders. Before cutting, fold the fabric with selvedges matching so it fits on the cutting mat. Cut the border strips across the fabric width; leave the selvedges on at this stage.

▼ *The quilt comes together in easy stages. The twelve patchwork blocks are framed by sashing strips and three borders, and simple machine quilting gives surface texture to the finished quilt.*

Assembling the quilt top

1 Cutting the sashing strips Fold fabric with selvedges matching so it fits on the cutting mat. Cut strips 9cm (3½in) wide across width of the fabric. Cut these into 31.5cm (12½in) long segments; you need 31 segments.

2 Preparing the four-patch squares Choose two fabrics. From each, cut two 5.25cm (2in) wide strips across the full fabric width. Right sides together, stitch the strips together in pairs. Press seam allowances towards darker fabric. Cut across into 40 5.25cm (2in) wide sections.

3 Stitching the four-patch squares Stitch the cut sections together in pairs to give 20 four-patch squares. The seam allowances will automatically lie in opposite directions to provide accurate matching of seams at the centre of each pieced square.

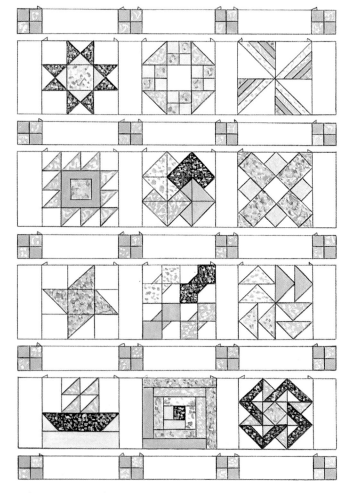

4 Stitching the sashing Lay the quilt blocks, sashing strips and four-patch squares on the floor in their final positions. Stitch vertical sashing strips to blocks, stretching or easing blocks a little if necessary to make them fit the sashing. Press seam allowances towards blocks.

5 Completing sashing Stitch the horizontal sashing strips to the four-patch squares in rows. Then stitch these to the rows of blocks with their sashing, matching the seamlines accurately. Press carefully.

6 Cutting the borders Cut across the full fabric width. *For the first border:* cut seven strips 9cm (3½in) wide. *For the second border:* cut seven strips 11.5cm (4½in) wide. *For the third border:* cut eight strips 14cm (5½in) wide.

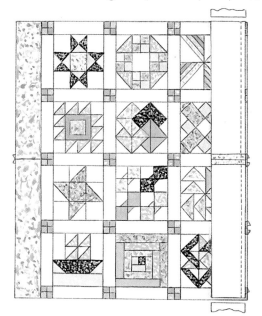

7 Stitching the first border Place two first border strips right sides together. Stitch across the short edges to give a strip 224cm (88in) long. Repeat with another two first border strips. Stitch one border to each side of the quilt, matching the seam to the centre of the quilt. Trim excess fabric. Press seam allowances towards the border.

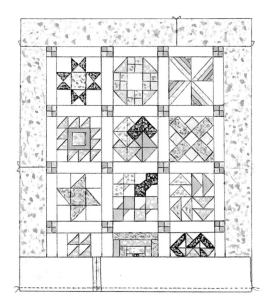

8 Completing the first border Join two first border strips as in step **7**. Stitch across the top edge, trim away the excess fabric, then join it to the remaining border strip. Finally, stitch it to the bottom of the quilt. Press.

9 Stitching the second and third borders Repeat steps **7-8** to attach the second and third border strips to the sides of the quilt. Press.

Machine quilting and adding the binding

The final stages of completing the quilt involve marking the quilting design on to the quilt top, tacking the quilt top, wadding and backing layers together, machine quilting the design and neatening the edges with binding.

The blocks are quilted using the patchwork as the stitching guide. Use a quilter's ruler and chalk or pencil in a colour that shows up well on the fabric to mark the diagonal grid on the borders and a quilting stencil to mark the design on the sashing. Choose a stencil which fits the width of the sashing and allows you to machine in a continuous flow. If you can't find one with a suitable corner design, use a simple motif such as a heart at each corner.

For the backing, use one of your patchwork fabrics or a toning fabric of the same weight. For wadding, light-weight 60g (2oz) polyester wadding is a good choice, as it is not too bulky to work with and is machine washable.

For machine quilting, you need to use a mercerized cotton thread in the bobbin in a colour to match the backing fabric; in the needle you need to use either a cotton thread to blend with the patchwork, or a fine, invisible nylon thread. Loosen the upper thread tension, if necessary, to prevent the bobbin thread from pulling through to the right side of the fabric. For the best results, use an even-feed foot attachment, which helps feed the layers through the machine evenly.

1 Preparing the quilt top for marking Press the quilt top and lay it out on a hard, flat surface. Tape the edges of the quilt at intervals to hold it taut.

2 Positioning the stencil Position the corner design on the four-patch squares first. Work out placement of design on sashing strips. Once you are happy with the effect, mark the design on to the strips through the stencil.

3 Marking the diagonal grid Using a quilter's ruler, mark a line at one corner at a 45 degree angle to edge of quilt top. Stop line at inner edge of first border. Continue marking parallel lines 10cm (4in) apart along one side of quilt. Repeat in opposite direction to form a diamond pattern. Continue diamond pattern all round the borders.

4 Preparing the quilt Tack the quilt top, wadding and backing together. Then follow page 82, step **3** to roll and fold the quilt, to make it manageable for machine quilting. As you work, support the quilt on your lap and on the work surface to the left and behind your sewing machine.

5 Working the machine quilting Starting with centre blocks, stitch-in-the-ditch along lines of the patchwork. Quilt marked design lines on the sashing as you complete each block. Continue working in this way from centre out towards edges. Finally, quilt the diagonal lines on the borders.

6 Preparing the binding strips Choose one of your patchwork fabrics, or a toning fabric, and fold it with the selvedges matching so that it fits on the cutting mat. Cut strips 4.5cm (1½in) wide across the width of the fabric. With right sides together, join the pieces together to make four strips long enough to go across the top and bottom and down the sides of the quilt.

7 Attaching the binding With right sides together and matching the raw edge of binding to edge of quilt top, pin the binding strips to the top and bottom edges of the quilt; stitch. Trim the wadding and backing fabric.

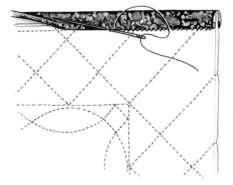

8 Slipstitching the binding Trim away excess binding strip at each end, then turn under 7.5mm (¼in) on edge of binding strip. Fold the strip to the back of the quilt and slipstitch in place over the line of machine stitching.

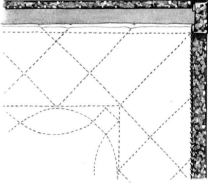

9 Completing the binding Pin and stitch the border strips to the sides of the quilt as in step **7**. Trim the binding strip to leave 1cm (½in) at each end. Turn under 7.5mm (¼in) on the edge of the strip, then fold in the ends. Fold the binding to the back of the quilt and slipstitch it in place across the ends and along the previous line of machine stitching.

Index

Picture Acknowledgements

Photographs: Page 7: Robert Harding Syndication/IPC Magazines Magazines(Chris Drake); Page 8(t): Robert Harding Syndication/IPC Magazines Magazines(Lucinda Symons); Page 8(b): Robert Harding Syndication/IPC Magazines Magazines(Dominic Blackmore); Page 9(cl): Robert Harding Syndication/IPC Magazines Magazines(Lucinda Symons); Page 9(bl): Robert Harding Syndication/IPC Magazines Magazines(Chris Drake); Page 9(r): Robert Harding Syndication/IPC Magazines Magazines(Trevor Richards); Page 10(t): Robert Harding Syndication/IPC Magazines Magazines (Lucinda Symons); Page 10(b): Worldwide Syndication; Page 11: Eaglemoss Publications/Graham Rae; Page 13-14: Eaglemoss Publications/Graham Rae; Page 15: Ariadne Holland; Page 16-17: Robert Harding Syndication/IPC Magazines Magazines; Page 18: Crowson; Page 19: Robert Harding Syndication/IPC Magazines Magazines; Page 20: Colefax & Fowler; Page 21-22: Robert Harding Syndication/IPC Magazines Magazines; Page 23: Romo Ltd; Page 24-25: Eaglemoss Publications/Steve Tanner; Page 27-28: Biggie Best/Sarah Flemimg; Page 29: Laura Ashley; Page 30-34: Robert Harding Syndication/IPC Magazines Magazines; Page 35: Ariadne Holland; Page 36-38: Eaglemoss Publications/Jez Hawley;

Page 39-42: Eaglemoss Publications/LizzieOrme; Page 43-46: Eaglemoss Publications/Paul Bricknell; Page 50: Eaglemoss Publications/George Taylor; Page 51: Ariadne Holland; Page 52: Eaglemoss Publications/Adrian Taylor; Page 53(t): Eaglemoss Publications/Adrian Taylor; Page 53(b): Ariadne Holland; Page 54: Eaglemoss Publications/Adrian Taylor; Page 55: Ariadne Holland; Page 56-57: Marie Claire Idées(Chabaneix/ Chabaneix); Page 58: Eaglemoss Publications/Graham Rae; Page 59: Elizabeth Whiting & Associates/Jean-Paul Bonhommet; Page 61-62: Eaglemoss Publications/Adrian Taylor; Page 63-65: Ariadne Holland; Page 65(b): Robert Harding Syndication/IPC Magazines Magazines(James Merrell); Page 66(t,c): Ariadne Holland; Page 66(b): Modes et Travaux; Page 71-74: Eaglemoss Publications/George Taylor; Page 77-80: Eaglemoss Publications/Steve Tanner; Page 83-84: Eaglemoss Publications/George Taylor; Page 87: Eaglemoss Publications/Lizzie Orme; Page 88: Eaglemoss Publications/Adrian Taylor; Page 89: Eaglemoss Publications/Lizzie Orme; Page 90: Eaglemoss Publications/Adrian Taylor; Page 91: Eaglemoss Publications/Steve Tanner; Page 92: Eaglemoss Publications/Adrian Taylor; Page 93-94: Eaglemoss Publications/Steve Tanner; Page 95: Eaglemoss Publications/Lizzie

Orme; Page 96: Eaglemoss Publications/Adrian Taylor; Page 97-99: Eaglemoss Publications/Lizzie Orme; Page 100-101: Eaglemoss Publications/Adrian Taylor; Page 102-103: Eaglemoss Publications/Lizzie Orme; Page 104-105(t): Eaglemoss Publications/Adrian Taylor; Page 105(b)-106: Eaglemoss Publications/Lizzie Orme; Page 107: Eaglemoss Publications/Steve Tanner; Page 108(t): Eaglemoss Publications/Adrian Taylor; Page 108(b): Eaglemoss Publications/Steve Tanner; Page 109: Eaglemoss Publications/Lizzie Orme; Page 110-111: Eaglemoss Publications/Adrian Taylor; Page 112: Eaglemoss Publications/Lizzie Orme; Page 113: Eaglemoss Publications/Paul Bricknell; Page 114: Eaglemoss Publications/Adrian Taylor; Page 115: Biggie Best: Page 117-118: Eaglemoss Publications/Adrian Taylor; Page 119: Eaglemoss Publications/Tony Chau; Page 120: Eaglemoss Publications/Adrian Taylor; Page 121-126: Eaglemoss Publications/Lizzie Orme.

Illustrations: Page 12-32: John Hutchinson; Page 34-38: Coral Mula; Page 40-42: John Hutchinson; Page 44-62: Coral Mula; Page 67-68: Sally Holmes; Page 69-86: Coral Mula; Page 89-94: John Hutchinson; Page 96-106: Coral Mula; Page 108: John Hutchinson; Page 110-126: Coral Mula.